GICHIGAMI HEARTS

Also by Linda LeGarde Grover

PUBLISHED BY THE UNIVERSITY OF MINNESOTA PRESS

The Road Back to Sweetgrass
In the Night of Memory
Onigamiising: Seasons of an Ojibwe Year

GICHIGAMI HEARTS

STORIES *and* HISTORIES
FROM MISAABEKONG

LINDA LeGARDE GROVER

UNIVERSITY *of* MINNESOTA PRESS
Minneapolis // London

Epigraph reprinted with permission from *The Dance Boots: Stories* by Linda LeGarde Grover (Athens: University of Georgia Press, 2010).

"The Stone Tomahawk" was previously published in a different form in *The State We're In*, edited by Annette Atkins and Deborah L. Miller (St. Paul: Minnesota Historical Society Press, 2010).

Photographs are courtesy of the author, unless credited otherwise.

Published by the University of Minnesota Press
111 Third Avenue South, Suite 290
Minneapolis, MN 55401-2520
http://www.upress.umn.edu

ISBN 978-1-5179-1193-5

A Cataloging-in-Publication record for this book is available from the Library of Congress.

Printed in the United States of America on acid-free paper

The University of Minnesota is an equal-opportunity educator and employer.

28 27 26 25 24 23   10 9 8 7 6 5 4 3 2

And so Elias joined his true love, Victoria,
and they joined the others who watch us
from far beyond where the sun sets,
the past that birthed the present
that even now births the future.
They pray as we pass into life,
they pray us through our lives,
they pray us as we pass out of life;
when we die, they pray our steps across the walk west.
Thus blessed, we live and die
in an air hung with their prayers,
the breath of their words on our faces and bodies,
their spirits among us,
trying to see and hear and understand.
Wegonen, what is it, we think.
Amanj i dash, and I wonder.
We ponder this all of our lives,
not realizing what we already know.

—ARTENSE GALLETTE

CONTENTS

Angelique LaVierge and her husband, George Danielson,
with daughters and grandchildren at their home
on Park Point in Duluth, circa 1905

PART OF A MASSIVE RIDGE of gabbro rock that extends southwest of Duluth and follows the north shore of Lake Superior into Canada, the Point of Rocks divides the city of Duluth in half.

The area around Duluth has been known by Ojibwe words that describe this terrain. One of these is Onigamiising, the place of the small portage, which refers to the five-mile-long sandbar not far from the Point of Rocks. Another is Misaabekong, the place of the giants. Standing on top of those walls of gabbro, or looking up at the mass of rock and trees from the valleys and lakeshore, we are standing among the giants.

In 1838, newlyweds Josepha Susan Neganigijigok and Gabriel Egomo LaVierge traveled from LaPointe, Wisconsin, on Madeline Island to Fond du Lac, the Ojibwe settlement next to the American Fur Post on the St. Louis River in Minnesota. Their first child, Angelique, was born in 1839 at the Fond du Lac settlement, in sight of the gabbro ridge before there was a

Duluth, or a State of Minnesota, before the lands of the Minnesota Arrowhead were lost under the terms of the 1854 Treaty.

That baby girl lived to be an old woman. Angelique's children and grandchildren scattered under federal removals and relocations and became part of the Bois Forte, Fond du Lac, and Grand Portage bands. She died in the West End neighborhood, in sight of the western side of the Point of Rocks, and is buried in the Park Hill cemetery, next to her husband, a Civil War veteran. During her lifetime, Angelique had moved from one end of Duluth to the other, never far from the gabbro ridge and the Point of Rocks.

We, the descendants, are of this land and story, and this land and story are of us. We are honored to live in this place of the giants.

PART I
POINT
OF ROCKS

GABBRO

HERE IN ONIGAMIISING—Duluth, Minnesota, the small city on the western tip of Lake Superior—a massive outcropping of gabbro rock, the Point of Rocks, divides the city in half. Never far from that uneven and rocky hill that affords views of Lake Superior to the east, and to the west, of Park Point peninsula and Lake Superior Harbor, to St. Louis Bay and then the St. Louis River, we Onigamiisingowininiwag, Native and non-Native, live surrounded by beauty created by the Great Spirit, the Creator, through the ages. This is both our history and our existence today.

Onigamiising is known by a few names besides that of Daniel Greysolon, Sieur du Lhut, the French explorer who arrived at this end of Lake Superior in 1679. Like other Europeans who made their way into the interior, he was looking for something—many were looking for areas rich in natural resources that could be harvested, especially furs, but I believe that a desire for peace and quiet, beauty, and setting foot on a land that other Europeans had never seen was also part of the quest. It is doubtful that he was surprised to find that there were already people living here: the Ojibwe who had themselves journeyed from the northeast coastal regions, from what is now northern New England, into Canada and Newfoundland. During the Great Migration of the Ojibwe, there were a number of places where people stopped and stayed, all spiritual and sacred because of their creation by the Great Spirit, the Creator, who sent the visions and dreams directing the journey. When Sieur du Lhut reached what is now the Fond du Lac neighborhood of far western Duluth, that place was already home to an established Ojibwe community. My ancestors, my father's grandparents and the generations preceding them, had traveled from the east on a route that followed the Great Lakes to Sault Ste. Marie, on the far eastern end of Lake Superior where it joins Lake Huron. Some family groups continued westward to LaPointe, the Ojibwe community on Madeline Island in Wisconsin, and some went further to Fond du Lac, at the western end of Lake Superior. Others traveled northward from Sault Ste. Marie to Fort Frances,

Ontario, and then south to Grand Portage, which is 150 miles northeast of present-day Duluth, and to the Bois Forte on Lake Vermilion, in northern Minnesota. At Fond du Lac, the LaVierges and LeGardes established lives and extended families that experienced upheavals, removals, returns, the breaking up of families, and the reconnection of families, as when my great-grandmother Lucy Ann married Muh-Quay-Mud and began their dynasty at Bois Forte, and when my grandmother Victoria and grandfather Elias, both students at the Vermilion Lake Indian School near Tower, Minnesota, met and joined families that had known and lived with one another for a very long time before European contact.

From the Point of Rocks, the view northeastward of Lake Superior stretches for many miles and fades into a horizon of lake and sky, and south-westward to the harbor, bay, and the St. Louis River where the waters narrow and the view fades to a gray-blue mist with outlines that cannot be clearly identified. I squint and think *There it is, Fond du Lac, I think that is it* and recall times I have been there—the Local 106 Painters Union picnics when I was a little girl, the dam, the fur post historical marker—and times and events that occurred before my time on Earth but that I feel just the same.

Not far from the base of Point of Rocks is a five-mile-long peninsula, Park Point, a natural sandbar that separates lake and natural harbor. The old Ojibwe and fur traders traveling by canoe portaged across that sand-bar on their way to, among other places, the American Fur Company Post, built in 1808 at Fond du Lac and abandoned in 1847. The shortest, easiest point to portage was close to today's downtown and Canal Park, a stretch of only about two blocks. Onigamiising refers to that place; the word trans-lates in English to "the place of the small portage." Another locative word for the Duluth area is Misaabekong, the place of the giants, which identifies the large ridge above the area out of which emerges the Point of Rocks. I have heard that the word *misaabekong* might have referred specifically to the Point of Rocks in the past, but have not been able to verify that in the stories from our Ojibwe tradition. It is interesting, I think, that American Indian names and words for places seem to be descriptive of the notable natural area, while so many American/English names for places bear a specific per-son's name: for example, Duluth.

"I betcha if you asked everybody in Duluth where the Point of Rocks is, you'd get a different answer from each person," my husband commented as we drove around the area one afternoon to see if there might be specific nat-ural boundaries. As we passed the outcropping off West First Street where for many years a large Taystee Bread sign overlooked Garfield Avenue, Rice's Point, and the Blatnik Bridge (aka "the High Bridge"), I answered, "I

Point of Rocks

betcher right." We both speak the same language because we are from the West End and West Duluth.

For me, the Point of Rocks is bounded by two avenues that ascend curving up each side from the bottom, Superior Street, to the top of the hill, holding the outcropping between them like a pair of cupped hands. Although the gabbro formation is a good mile and a half wide at the top, on Michigan Street it is just a few blocks in width; for nearly a century and a half there has been a small settlement in a scooped-out area that is usually called Glen Place and has its own story within the history of the Duluth area. The Italian immigrant community that lived there called the settlement "Piedmont" after their homeland. Originally, both of the avenues that wrapped the outcropping were named Piedmont, too, and eventually the eastern one was renamed Mesaba Avenue while the western one kept the name Piedmont Avenue.

Greenery grows from the cracks and spaces of the Point of Rocks where the rock has eroded or split and soil has blown in. Here, since long before the Ojibwe, long before the Native people who lived here before the Ojibwe, certainly long before Duluth, and longer ago than that—even before the glacier that covered this place ten thousand years ago, before the glacier melted and the area was covered by water and there was no surface land or small portage at all—the outcropping has seen a great many stories and knows a great many secrets. Our Ojibwe and, in a broader sense, Anishinaabe history is a layering of our stories over that land and lakescape, and our traditional teachings that encourage us to strive for a life of balance are a reflection of that. Point of Rocks, surely an intended work of the Creator for our natural world, may not have been intended as a separation so much as a tangible fulcrum of hope for balanced lives across and throughout Onigamiising's neighborhoods.

The Point of Rocks bears scars from two attempted blastings, once during the 1870s exploration for gold and minerals and then again during World War I, the second time an attempt to straighten out Superior Street. Both were unsuccessful, even futile, but the breaking up of the gabbro created by the search for gold created a small valley scooped out at the bottom of the outcropping. The Italian immigrants who came to Duluth in the early twentieth century settled in the lush greenness of the valley, sheltered somewhat on three sides from the iciness of the northern winter wind. That valley, neatly contained between Superior Street and First Street, was called "Little Italy" and later "the hollow" and Glen Place or "the Glen," a neighborhood that expanded up the hill as it grew. As part of the urban-renewal programs of the 1960s, the houses in the Glen were purchased and most were torn down. Apartment buildings rose up on the Superior Street entrance, but much of the rest of the Glen has continued to return to greenery and rock. Today the area above the Glen, the West Hillside, is anchored to the geography and history of Duluth, as are we all, by that massive outcropping of gabbro and the lifeblood of the Piedmont descendants who built roads, homes, schools, and churches.

Here in Onigamiising most of the neighborhoods in our 13 x 3-mile city abut the lake or are within a mile or two of water. Many of our poorest areas have million-dollar views of Lake Superior. Across that thirteen miles, some us live east of the Point of Rocks, some west, some in the apartment buildings that have been built in the Glen, and some perched above that mass of gabbro and greenery. We live within sight and shadow of a terrain that has demonstrated a strength far beyond mankind's pitiful tinkerings, an immovable and imponderable beauty that will continue to exist, with its stories and secrets, in the animate state in which the Ojibwe people and language regard *asin*, or stone.

The old Ojibweg used to say that a long time ago the people and the animals could talk with one another. Perhaps even longer ago, the people could communicate with the trees and plants, with the water, and also with the stones, and perhaps that is one reason why in the Ojibwe language the stone is considered to be animate. Perhaps the stones still do speak but we don't hear or understand.

AN OLD STORY

THERE IS A STORY about the Point of Rocks I heard some time ago, one of life's mysteries, that might be cleared up and understood if the gabbro would speak and was willing to tell me, which it might do someday. The story takes place in fairly recent times and is not one of the old stories of the creation of the Earth, yet I feel that it must tie in with those stories. Its brevity generates wonderment and a human desire to know—in Ojibwe fashion, the listener and reader practice the virtue of realizing that knowledge is not there just for the pursuing, that if our understanding is meant to be, it will happen when it should. And yet, in our pitiful way, we cannot help but wonder.

It goes like this: one of the times the rock was being blasted, near where the Bethel Society building is today, between Superior and First Streets, a large crack opened and an Anishinaabe man dressed in old-style clothes stepped out. He looked all around him and then walked away, just walked away.

Dash mih sa'iw noongoom. And that is all there is for now.

BIMOSEWIN

FROM *the* BETHEL *to the* UNION GOSPEL MISSION

DULUTH'S FIRST STREET passes through many neighborhoods that are diverse in their buildings, financial resources, and histories. Bisecting Mesaba Avenue, First Street winds westward around the natural formations of gabbro until it reaches Duluth's West End and then continues for miles, sometimes straight, sometimes curved and even interrupted, through the western neighborhoods. Eastward, First Street lies in a straight line through the downtown and the Central and East Hillside neighborhoods, and, finally, to Duluth's East End. Much of Duluth's street life has been concentrated for more than a century on the ten-block stretch of downtown First Street between the Union Gospel Mission near Third Avenue East and the Bethel, near Eighth Avenue West. Both street missions were founded by Duluth religious and civic leaders to provide a place to sleep, a meal, a prayer service, and some social services for Great Lakes seamen, lumberjacks, and other transient men. Today, I suppose, they no longer require a prayer service before food and rest; the populations they serve have expanded and they work with other governmental social-service entities, but they still provide faith-based services.

The Bethel building was built in 1912, a three-story L-shaped building that faces northeast toward Lake Superior and the North Shore. A few years ago, the long-dark amber light at its apex—a beacon meant to guide rough men from the freighters and streets to a meal, a religious service, a washup, and a bed—was restored.

The Union Gospel Mission, founded in 1922, began in a storefront building on Second Avenue East. The mission moved down the block and across the street to a larger space twenty years ago, but the original building stands, looking more run-down but otherwise not much changed from October 1970 when the minister sent us a sympathy card after my grandfather was found fallen in an alley nearby and brought to the hospital, where he died of pneumonia. The minister wrote in the card that he knew my grandfather and was sorry he had passed. It was a kind thing to do, and so normal-seeming, a card sent to a family whose grandfather had died. Our grief was complicated and lasted a long time, through to today and as long as anyone will remember him—as we, his descendants with those memories age and pass, those memories will pass too, which calls up another kind of grief.

I sometimes picture time as a slide rule—dates and lives coinciding and paralleling as we move that mathematical tool back and forth, past to present, understanding groupings, sets, and patterns but not quite how it all fits together. The Bethel Society was formed around the time of the first attempted blasting of the Point of Rocks. The Bethel building opened for business the same year Uncle Bob was born in Chippewa City, an Ojibwe community a mile and a half northeast of Grand Marais, Minnesota, on the shore of Lake Superior. By 1922, when the Union Gospel Mission opened, Bob and his little brothers were at the Indian boarding school in Red Lake, Minnesota, and their parents had moved from the Grand Portage reservation to Duluth after their house burned down.

My grandfather Elias LeGarde, who was born in 1900 and died in 1970, was one of the many men who regularly ate, listened to sermons, cleaned up, and slept at the street missions in the 1950s and 1960s. During my grandfather's time, every day the First Street people wandered between the Gospel Mission and the Bethel; some lived in rooms above stores downtown, some were between places and needed a place to eat and sleep. As I remember it, they seemed to know one another: on hot days they stayed on the shaded side of the street, on cold days they huddled in doorways, between buildings, or in alleyways, smoking cigarettes if they had them, moving a little and shuffling their feet to stay warm. Occasionally, they panhandled. Not everybody was there every day; many worked, often seasonal jobs at the scrap yards, on the docks, on the boats. My grandfather spent many of his winters at the county work farm. He could handle horses, my dad said. He had learned to play the trumpet at the Pipestone Indian Boarding School and traveled for a while with a circus band, where he had been an Indian cowboy and could do rope tricks, like Will Rogers, my dad said.

There were a lot of businesses, and a lot of bars, on First Street. Although it was a little shabbier than Superior Street, Duluth's main downtown street, there was a lot going on. My mother's engagement ring came from Garon Brothers, a jewelry store on First Street since 1907. That was in 1950. In 1997, my daughter married a young man who worked in that jewelry store, which was still owned by the Garon family.

When I was eighteen, I was hired by the telephone company, Northwestern Bell, where I was trained to be a toll/long-distance operator, work that I enjoyed. Whenever my shift ended too late in the evening for the bus, my dad would pick me up. I waited inside the glass doors at Bell, watching for his red truck. At that time of night I could see men walking west toward the Bethel or east to the Union Gospel Mission, just a few feet from me, or across the street passing an office machine company, with an Olivetti Girl poster in the window. She looked so happy to be able to work on one of those typewriters.

My grandfather was one of those men who walked along First Street between the Bethel and the Union Gospel mission. I never saw him through the glass doors of Northwestern Bell. At eighteen, I didn't understand much about our history yet but knew that there was more to the story. I know now that my grandfather and the other *niijiis*, the downtown and West End friends by histories and hearts, walked in the very footsteps of the Anishinaabe man who emerged from the cracks of gabbro when it was blown open.

Then, in the midst of several semidramas and semitraumas of the young womanhood of the times, I moved to Chicago, then back to Duluth, to Chicago, to Duluth, lost. I was in Duluth when my grandfather died and was able to go to his funeral.

Three years later, I was back on First Street, married, pregnant, and working as a teller at a credit union where our lunch breaks were an hour long, which left time to kill. Most days I took a walk, usually six or eight blocks eastward on First Street toward the Union Gospel Mission and back, my steps taking me past Northwestern Bell and the new YMCA, several bars, and Garon Brothers Jewelers, past two grocery stores, a bakery, and many small shops where most of the buildings rented rooms or apartments, and past *niijii* after *niijii* who had nowhere in particular to go and so moved more slowly than me. Occasionally, a *niijii* would nod at me as though we knew each other, which in truth we did.

One cloudy lunch break when I passed by the Union Gospel Mission I slowed my steps slightly and looked as indirectly and inconspicuously as I could through the sheer curtains that covered the bottom half of the storefront windows. I was not really looking for my grandfather since he had died two years earlier, and yet I was. Inside were two long tables and several rows of metal folding chairs with a few men sitting there, waiting for the Bible reading, then something to eat, I suppose. Meals were free at the Union Gospel Mission, and so were beds, first come first served, on a nightly basis. In the front half of the first floor, the storefront, men could gather to visit and for some respite from walking the sidewalks on First Street, the concrete always hard on the feet and legs of men who were often tired and discouraged, terribly cold in winter and burning through the soles of their shoes in summer.

Prayer services at the Union were held in this storefront, and at lunch and suppertime food was brought out from the back and set out on a long table. The men ate sitting on the folding chairs. Evenings, those who were going to sleep there were allowed upstairs, where there were rooms with single cots, and a washroom where they could clean up and wash their other set of underwear and socks, if they had them, in the sinks. In those days it seemed that only men ate and slept at the Bethel and the Union Gospel Mission, and so many of them were aging Native men. Where Native women on the streets went for food or a place to sleep was disturbing to think about. There were things that women desperate for those basics had to do to obtain them or do without.

The clouds moved, unblocking the sun; as my shadow moved across the sheer white curtains, one of the men looked up at the windows. Feeling intrusive, I moved on.

Our first daughter was born. We bought a car and a couch with a matching chair and it was a nice life there in our basement apartment in the West End, on the other side of the Point of Rocks. My husband Tim worked for my dad, who was a painting contractor. I drove him to work on days I wanted the car. One day, I brought him his lunch at the Bethel, when LeGarde Painting was working on a free/volunteer job, a shuffleboard court on the gymnasium floor. Tim was spending the day prepping the concrete floor for the paint. I had dressed our baby girl in her blue polka-dot dress and ruffled white bonnet. The gym was dark in contrast to the bright sunlight outside, and I stepped carefully over the areas he had already etched and handed him sandwiches and coffee, telling him I would be sure to get to the electric company to pay our bill before they closed for the day. Back outside, several *niijiis* leaning against the railing outside the doorway glanced indirectly at me; one nodded politely. They were no doubt thinking "rich Indian girl"—a term from those times that is both loaded and complex. As I buckled the belt across the baby in her blue plastic Infanseat and got into our nearly new Pinto, I felt overdressed and overblessed. We headed our separate ways, me luxuriously driving west on First Street to Piedmont Avenue and the West End, the men on foot east to downtown.

There is something of the man who walked away from the rock blasting in all of us; some have been luckier than others since then. There is an Ojibwe word, *aaniish*, that offers the question "why?" My aunt told me the word is not used often because it can be construed as disrespectful and even unseemly, but I think that it is appropriate here. *Aaniish?*

FROM THE ROCKS TO THE DOCKS

SUPERIOR STREET RUNS EAST TO WEST across the bottom of Glen Place, the semiscooped-out hollow at the base of the Point of Rocks formed by the blastings that failed more than a century ago. At each end of Glen Place is an avenue that runs from Superior Street up the hill. The Point of Rocks is wrapped by these, Mesaba on the eastern side and Piedmont on the western. East of Mesabi is Duluth's downtown, and in its irregular winding around rock formations Piedmont Avenue cups Goat Hill, the neighborhood on the steep western side of the outcropping.

Piedmont is an area of Italy, and I have heard that one of the names Glen Place has been known by was Little Piedmont, likely because of the settlement of Italian immigrants there. As it winds up the hill, ending at the Haines Road, which is the boundary between Duluth and Hermantown, Piedmont Avenue is quite steep in some places. Until the grain trucks on their way to the port terminal down past the bottom of Piedmont were rerouted, brake issues caused terrible accidents with some regularity, and a gas station on the curve at Ninth Street and Piedmont was demolished at least twice.

That gas station was a block below Ensign Elementary School, which occupied the western half of the square block between Tenth and Eleventh Streets on Piedmont Avenue. Ensign opened in 1908 in a four-room wood-frame building, the old Monroe school that had been moved from the lower West End. That building was torn down in the 1920s and replaced by a brick building. I was a student at Ensign for fifth and sixth grades, and my younger brothers and sisters attended that school until it closed in 1979.

Teachers who had been at Ensign for a long time talked sometimes about the days when there was a school newspaper. This story, and their nostalgia for the days when Ensign was a much better school with much better students (they wanted to be sure that we knew this), had become part of the tapestry of the history of what was called the "upper West End"—anything above Tenth Street, it seemed, was a little tonier than everything below. By the time the LeGarde children got to Ensign, the building and the neighborhood were getting a little tired out. The return of the school paper, and the traditions that surrounded it (what those traditions were was never specified), would help restore Ensign's and the neighborhood's glory days. I remember that some of the younger children were afraid of one or two of the longtime teachers, who could be less than kind—one of them still dressed in the clothing styles of the 1930s and wore her hair in little sausage curls, probably from rubber or kid curlers. The janitor, however, was a benevolent older man with a lot of white hair, like Santa Claus or a grandfather. I believe he loved his job, and the children. His work outfit, matching dark shirt and pants, always looked pressed.

I thought the school was pretty nice, like a museum, although a little dark and shadowy; the woodwork, and there was a lot of it, was lovely and polished, the etched glass of many-paned doors to the classrooms like new, and the main stairway, with iron railings that split and curved (girls to the left, boys to the right) was airy and graceful. I climbed them to the second floor and then walked down the always-immaculate hallway floor that squeaked to the sixth-grade classroom in the corner at the end, saying a little prayer that the teacher, a temperamental woman who had been president of the Girls Club in her days at Denfeld High School before the First World War, would be having a good day (what made her days good or bad was a mystery), which might trickle down to us.

Difficult though she might be, it was from that teacher that I first heard about the legendary Ensign school newspaper from the past glory days of the school, *La Monte News,* and the story behind its name. I remember nothing about *La Monte News,* though I believe an edition was pulled together a few years later and then the project was abandoned, but I have not forgotten the story of how the newspaper came by its name. That story, mysteriously significant and profound, connected the man who emerged from the rock blastings at Glen Place to the western side of the Point of Rocks and to Ensign school, and to the relationships between Indigenous people, land, and the passing of history and knowledge from one generation to the next.

The narrative—spoken by a teacher long tired of her job and the limitations life imposed on a president of the Denfeld Girls Club, a smart young suffragist whose options were marriage, nursing, or teaching—was communicated in an unintendedly camp fashion; I believe that at the conclusion she may have placed a hand to her brow, palm down, looking toward the sunset, Indian-fashion. That didn't matter—the story was magical, and it stayed with me.

Long ago, an American Indian man walked from the direction of Goat Hill and the Point of Rocks to Ensign School, where he approached the teachers and students and, while gesturing toward the hills, began to speak to them in a language they didn't understand. "Is that where you are from?" a teacher asked. Another teacher thought he heard the words *la monte* and asked, "Do you mean the mountain?" The man spoke again, with some urgency, but they could not communicate and so he continued walking. They never saw him again, but the story wasn't forgotten, and when Ensign school created a newspaper, probably in the 1930s or 1940s, they titled it *La Monte News.*

This is one of those stories that has no specific dates, or names of people who were present. When did the Native man walk up to the children and teachers of Ensign school—was it around the time of the second blasting at Glen Place? What was he trying to tell them?

All fourteen of the LeGarde children attended Ensign. The first, I was there for only two years and didn't like it much, but eventually the family established our presence and belonging, and we were sad to see it close in 1979. The fixtures, including the beautiful glass-paned oak classroom doors, were auctioned off. My parents bought one of those doors and used it to replace our old front door, which whistled and howled on windy nights. Not long after Ensign closed, a mysterious fire burned the empty building beyond salvage, and it was torn down. Today, several affordable housing units stand on the site of the building and the playground that in winter had been a skating rink, attended by an old man who shoveled coal into a small stove inside the wooden warming shack.

With Ensign gone, the story of the Native man who walked from over the hill has been remembered and passed down by fewer people every year; that does not, however, diminish its existence or its significance. The stories and what is real are larger, stronger, and more permanent than our frail chain of human existence.

Mewinzha, a long time ago, a Native man emerged from the blasting site at the bottom of the Point of Rocks and walked away. *Debwe,* this is the truth. *Gaye mewinzha,* and also a long time ago, a Native man walked—on pathways, roadside, perhaps even over streetcar tracks—from the near-black rock, brush, and trees that cover the west side of the Point of Rocks to Ensign Elementary School, midway up Piedmont Avenue, named for the Italian immigrants who settled in the wilds of the first attempted blasting. On foot he was walking, and spoke to teachers and schoolchildren, surely all of them now in the next world, in the language of the people who had traveled to this place hundreds of years ago, during the Great Ojibwe Migration. *Gaye debwe;* this is the truth also.

That they couldn't understand each other was perhaps, as the old-time Ojibwe would say, meant to be.

ANISHINAABE RELATIVES AND HOLY PLACES

THE MASSIVE RIDGE that runs southwest of Duluth northward into Canada is significant to the Ojibwe people both historically and spiritually. Like everything else in creation, including you and me, it is part of something much larger than even itself. There are a number of places along the ridge, including the Point of Rocks, the basin that is Onigamiising, and the North Shore of Lake Superior, that are of particular sacredness. There is no man-made signage, nor are there historical markers to identify these places; nevertheless, their locations and histories are shared in the proper manner within these regions. In Anishinaabe tradition, knowledge has been cared for and passed down from generation to generation by way of the oral tradition. One of the strengths of this way of teaching and learning is that no single person knows all things; rather, many people know parts of the story. This means that the worldview and teachings are woven into the tribes, communities, and families, a tapestry of knowledge.

The locations of places that are particularly sacred are known and shared in the ways that are the creation and sacred stories: one person might know one story, or some, but no one person would know all. It was not until I became an older person myself that I really had a feel for this. Around the time I reached middle age, my father and a few elder relatives, all now in the next world, pointed out a few of these places to me. We didn't take a special drive to do that, or make a pilgrimage; they simply told me as we passed by, or stopped, or when we were talking. They mentioned these important things while we were eating fried eggs and potatoes, or walking to a gas station with a tire that had just gotten flat, or were on our way to pick up my mother after a hockey game at the Duluth Arena-Auditorium where she worked at Concession Stand 5.

Sometimes I visit these places to just be there, to breathe the air and feel the ground, the grass and weeds, exposed black gabbrous rock, or gravel, or blacktop, or concrete that so many others before me stood upon. I might offer tobacco, or say a quick conscious prayer. Other times, as I drive through town I acknowledge these places I pass by with a remembrance of those who have left a history so real that I can almost see it. How honored I feel to be part of something larger than myself, a chain of Anishinaabe existence that has remained unbroken, against the odds.

And every time I leave the house, it is there, that sacredness inseparable from place, whether I remember to think about it or not.

Duluth's West End neighborhood has not ever been a upscale place, but it has been a part of Duluth since the city was incorporated in 1857. The neighborhood runs from the west side of the Point of Rocks to the Ore Docks, around Thirtieth Avenue West, and from the lake up to the Skyline Boulevard, which was the stony rim of the lake formed millions of years ago by a glacier that later on melted to become Lake Superior. Looking west from the Skyline you can see the West End below, and beyond that West Duluth, Norton Park, Riverside, and even past that in the haze if you squint a little; I tell myself that I might be seeing even farther, to Morgan Park, Gary/New Duluth, and the Fond du Lac neighborhood, the last one in Duluth's city limits.

The West End has never been known as prosperous, but it has its own small business district and small neighborhoods. Many of my relatives have lived there over the past century and a half—my grandmother's grandmother Angelique LaVierge, who was born in 1839 in the Ojibwe settlement in today's Fond du Lac neighborhood, across the St. Louis River from the American Fur Post. Angelique lived with her husband George Washington Danielson and relatives on Superior Street in the West End when they were elderly. They died there and are buried in the Forest Park cemetery, out near Hunters Park in eastern Duluth. George was a Civil War veteran, and there is a section of the cemetery set aside for the men who had served in the Union Army. Two years after he died, the family, wanting Angelique and George together, bought two plots side by side in a regular section, and that is where they rest today, his Grand Army of the Republic headstone marking his grave and green grass on hers.

When I was a young woman, the West End had four major furniture stores, a J. C. Penney, a hobby shop, several clothing stores, a drugstore, a Ben Franklin, a shoe store, two grocery stores, and a couple dozen mom-and-pop corner stores. It had a photography studio, several doctors' and dentists' offices, restaurants, rooming houses and apartments above the businesses, and quite a number of bars. The area has gone through some tough times both before and since those days, and more often than not during its history things have looked like the business district is barely hanging on. However, it never really closes up. In the mid-1960s the half-mile-or-so stretch underwent some renewals: curbs were re-poured into curves to slow vehicle traffic and encourage a sort of wandering for pedestrians, some trees were planted into holes cut in the sidewalks, and the business association proclaimed the district with new signs: "The Friendly West End." Those signs are still there today, more than a half century later. The area really was a bustling place in those days. On Saturdays the sidewalks were packed and we really enjoyed ourselves. The new name really suited the place.

Friendly though it is, the Friendly West End still had its challenges: old buildings and infrastructure, tougher elements in the several bars, the medical offices closing up because of the competition of larger clinics. Clyde Iron Works, a heavy industrial fabricator, closed and was vacant for years; other industries did the same. The mom-and-pop stores vanished, all at once, it seemed, and not long after them, the grocery stores. When the furniture stores began to fail, it really looked like the end—all of Duluth had shopped the Big Four—but now, once again, the West End has begun to grow back, like a plant that blooms again after a trimming.

Some years ago, one of our classmates from Denfeld High School—my husband and I went to Denfeld and graduated together, we are of old-time Duluth, after all—thought that the neighborhood beyond the business district could use a little classing up. He proposed a new name: Lincoln Park. This was a little confusing for people at first because the West End does have a park called Lincoln Park, a lovely, wild place, but we supported him because although most of us have moved up the hill and out of the West End, he has stayed there and has really shown a commitment to the community. I still call the entire area, business district and neighborhoods, the West End, and there are many people like my dad and his friends who just could not bring themselves to use the new name. I myself am for anything that dresses the place up. Once, when driving through the business district, I used the term "gentrification" in a hopeful and optimistic statement to someone I know who loves old Duluth charm but is one of the newer people, not originally from here. She looked horrified—the concept meant different things to each of us, I suppose.

The newer merchants and businesses who are revitalizing our friendly West End have made an effort to keep the integrity of the lovely old-fashioned storefronts and interiors in their renovations. I love what they have been doing—it looks like home. They have begun to call the Friendly West End business district the Lincoln Park Craft District. I don't use that term myself, but must give credit to their efforts. This current cycle of renewal from restaurants, first one and then others following, many owned by the same stalwart family, has created some stylish places to eat that attract people from other parts of Duluth, both east and west of the Friendly West End, which is needed for this greatly loved place to survive. The work they have done to make good use of historical architectures and ambiances where that is possible has been a labor of love. I was in one of those places not long ago, the Corktown Deli—not my first visit there, but one that made me think and appreciate. My husband and I got our sandwiches and sat at the counter that was up against the storefront windows. It is the West End, after all, where we both lived when we were kids and young parents, and we wanted to watch the world go by in the way we would have on Saturdays when we were kids. At the table next to us was a woman I know from the University of Minnesota Duluth (UMD), having lunch with her children. Now, I knew that she lived on the other side of town, far past the Point of Rocks, and I was really pleased to see her there. We chatted a bit and then she said, "It is beautiful here, isn't it? Eating here with the view of that beautiful bluff."

The West End had a bluff? Where? I looked and, sure enough, the bluff she was talking about was Goat Hill, which is the west side of the Point of Rocks. Goat Hill is a steep little neighborhood, both its Piedmont Avenue border and the streets off Piedmont that run up the Point of Rocks hillside. There are some good stories from that area. One that I especially like is about a man who was changing a tire; when he set it down, it started rolling and he couldn't keep up as the rolling tire gathered speed and rolled for blocks, and he chased it calling out to warn anybody in the way. Driving the streets on Goat Hill can be hazardous in winter, walking them quite a workout in any season. And yet there are many houses there, most at least a century old. And from the steepness of Goat Hill there is a view of the Lake Superior harbor, the West End, and far beyond that to a blue-green-gray blur that is far western Duluth and the Fond du Lac neighborhood, where my great-great-grandmother Lucy was born in 1839 to young parents who had journeyed there from LaPointe, on Madeline Island, in northern Wisconsin. "It is pretty, isn't it," I answered, and it was indeed beautiful, brilliant green grass, bushes and trees growing out of the dark gray rocks, an occasional roof dotting the side of the hill. The sky was a bright blue, the sun was out, and there we were sitting in the beautiful, friendly West End eating lunch and looking out the storefront window. We were a block from where my grandmother's grandparents Angelique and George had lived their last days, with their younger relatives who would continue their story, and on down to me eating a roast beef sandwich on that lovely afternoon. We were a half block from the apartment building, still standing though in rough shape, where my grandmother and her children, my dad and his brothers and sister, lived. Down the street were two of the bars, still operating, where my dad shined shoes for five cents, where he and his sister sold willow baskets made by their mother for fifty cents (a handmade Ojibwe basket like those might sell for more than a hundred dollars today), and we were within a mile of places that relatives, some from so long ago they can be called ancestors, lived, worked, had families, had struggles and joys big and small. We couldn't see them and I supposed they couldn't see us but we are all real, our lives' stories layered in the palimpsest that is the West End.

GRANDPARENTS

I HAVE A PHOTOGRAPH of my aunt Carol when she was about ten years old taken on Third Street in the West End, likely by my grandmother, her aunt Vickie. In it are Carol, her mother Jessie (who was my great-aunt), some sisters and cousins, and far in the background, Goat Hill and the Point of Rocks. Carol is in the front, the smallest girl. She looks happy and full of life, just as she did decades later when she was a young elder and I a young mother, the evening we sat by my uncle Tommy's little campfire at the Ni-Mi-Win powwow held in the Duluth Bayfront Park, the Point of Rocks looming to our backs and in front of us the Aerial Lift Bridge, built at the dugout Onigamiising, the place of the small portage that made life a little easier for travelers long ago. Tommy had set up a tent where he would sleep during the nights of Ni-Mi-Win; inside, my cousin Bob was dressing for Grand Entry, to be held at "seven o'clock SHARP!" as the announcer said over the loudspeaker, making everybody laugh.

Carol and I were the only people sitting at the fire. And she began to talk.

"Can you see there's a house down there, about a block on the other side of the bridge? Did you know that house was your great-great-grandmother's house? You didn't? Well, she was a LaVierge, and she born at Fond du Lac, the old Fond du Lac not where the reservation is now where the people got moved, and her mother and dad came there from LaPointe, that big village on Madeline Island, in Wisconsin, do you know about that? Well, that was a long time ago; you ought to know some of these things. . . ." She spoke for a few minutes, then Bob emerged from the tent dressed in his regalia, black velvet beaded with Ojibwe-style flowers, vines, and leaves, and a fur hat. Bob is a poet, with an Ojibwe soul—much of his outfit had been made and beaded by his mother, my aunt Patsy, when he was a little boy. She had reworked and refitted the beaded pieces as he grew; when she died, too young, he was a young adult. All of this was with him as he smiled in his serious way at us; he was proud, humble, and clearly moved, his preparations of prayer while he dressed surrounding the very air around him.

"Is it seven o'clock sharp yet?" he asked.

We walked to the powwow circle and watched Bob take his place with the men's traditional dancers. Carol said that I should dance, that I should have a powwow dress, and then I could dance with her. A ribbon skirt, she thought, with leggings and a shawl. She would call me about that.

"And I'll tell you more about your grandmother, too, and our family, things you should know," she said.

It wasn't much past seven o'clock sharp when Grand Entry started. During an intertribal I danced, though I didn't have an outfit. And it wasn't much after that Ni-Mi-Win powwow that she kept her promise and called me to talk, to tell me the colors she had dreamed for my dress and leggings, to ask me how I was doing now that I was taking a college class, and to tell me stories about our family. As did the fictional Artense DuCharme and Aunt Shirley in the fiction I would come to write, Carol's task was to remember by heart and teach by rote, mine to learn by rote and remember by heart. In the years since, those stories have unfolded again and again in front of me, her memory of all she had listened to and remembered during her lifetime accurate and true.

Nokomis

When Angelique LaVierge Danielson, my great-great-grandmother, was born in 1839 in Fond du Lac, the American Fur Post was struggling as the fur trade bottomed out in Europe and America. Built by J. J. Astor in 1816, it would fold in 1847. Angelique was born before the land cessions and reservations established by the 1854 treaty, before the removal of the Fond du Lac Natives to the Fond du Lac Reservation twenty miles to the southwest, before there was a Duluth, before there was a State of Minnesota. Her parents, Gabriel Egomo LaVierge and Neganigijigokwe (Josepha; Susan) were born at LaPointe, on Madeline Island, one of the seven sacred stopping places of the Ojibwe during the Great Migration from the east. Madeline Island became a hub for the Ojibwe Nation: in tribal oral histories, the time from when the Ojibwe arrived until the fur trade led to an implosion and reduction of that community is known as the Golden Age of the Ojibwe, a time of peace and prosperity.

Gabriel and Neganigijigokwe were married in 1838 in LaPointe by Father Baraga, a Slovenian missionary who traveled extensively in his missionary work through the Lake Superior regions of Sault Ste. Marie, LaPointe, and the North Shore. During a time of illness at the Grand Portage Reservation, Father Baraga and a guide traveled by canoe from LaPointe to help care for the sick, nearly losing their lives during a rough storm. They landed at what is now Schroeder, Minnesota, where the Temperance River runs into Lake Superior. A cross commemorates the place of the landing.

The LaVierges moved to Fond du Lac, likely because of opportunities with the American Fur Post, and that is where their children were born. Although Gabriel is buried in the cemetery at LaPointe, the location of Neganigijigokwe's death and burial is not known. Angelique, their oldest daughte, married a white man, George Washington Danielson, in 1854, the year of the land cessions treaty. In that time of removal and turmoil, Angelique and her husband moved to Michigan. He served in the Union Army during the Civil War. Sometime after the war ended, they moved to Duluth, where as part of his scrip he was given land on Onigamiising, the Place of the Small Portage, just blocks from where the lift bridge stands today. The house he built is still there—many of his and Angelique's descendants lived there over many years, until the house passed out of family ownership.

In reading what I have written, this all looks so simple, so orderly, although the opposite is the truth. As part of the 1854 treaty, reservation lands were established and tribal people removed to much smaller tracts; the names of my family's relatives, some of which are the same names as of current generations, are on the removal and relocation lists. On the reservations, they experienced the difficulties of smaller areas to hunt, fish, gather, and harvest; their children were removed (that word again) and sent to boarding schools that attempted to solve the "Indian problem" by assimilating them into a facsimile of majority American life. Like many people, Angelique and George moved around, too—Duluth to Fond du Lac to northern Minnesota to Canada, back and forth. Their daughter Lucy Ann married Mah-Quay-Mud, Robert McKoy of the Bois Forte Band of the Lake Vermilion area. Their children were then Bois Forte members and were assigned land allotments at Nett Lake, twenty miles or so west of Orr, Minnesota.

Victoria Mellisa McKoy was my grandmother. She was born in Fort Frances (as far as we can establish) or perhaps Tower in February or October of 1890 or 1891, and attended an Indian boarding school in Fort Frances run by the Catholic church. When the U.S. government school at Tower opened in the late 1890s, she became a student there. It was at Vermilion Lake Indian School that she met her first husband, Martin Drouillard of the Grand Portage Reservation, and also her second husband, my grandfather Elias LeGarde (LaGarde; Lagard). All of her Drouillard children attended Indian boarding schools; her two youngest, my father Jerry and my uncle Tommy, did not. They were born in 1929 and 1931, right after the 1928 Merriam Report that led to the dismantling of the boarding school system. My dad talked sometimes about the pressure their mother had been under to

Children and staff at the Vermilion School, circa 1910

send them, and that she made all the effort she possibly could to keep them. I wondered how that could work; in one of our conversations, Carol told me that "she hid those little boys."

Mishoomis

My grandmother's life was not easy—my grandfather's was much harder. One factor in this was the regular, even constant, movement of Indian people from homeland to reservation, which was followed by removals (federally mandated relocations) to White Earth Reservation in western Minnesota, which was intended to eventually become one large reservation that would house all Ojibwe people, after all other Ojibwe reservations were closed and the lands used for homesteading, farming, or logging. Elias's grandmother, Amelia Vanoss, was born in 1845 to Leondre Vanoss, a Canadian, and NeZho-Dain (Angeline). His grandfather, Michael (Mitchell; Mitchle) LeGarde, was born in northern Wisconsin. LeGarde family members lived in Fond du Lac as well as the White Earth Reservation in western Minnesota. Their son, Louis, married Ella Thompson, of the Fond du Lac band.

Ella was one of many people from Fond du Lac who had been removed to the White Earth Reservation after the 1854 treaty. After her marriage to Louis LeGarde, they at some time moved to Mountain Iron, on Minnesota's Iron Range (although they parted company, they seem to have stayed not far from each other and eventually moved to Duluth); my grandfather Elias was born in Mountain Iron, or Iron. As a small boy at the Vermilion Lake Indian School he met my grandmother Victoria, who, after she finished school, stayed on to work as a helper with the younger children. It was years later, after Victoria and Martin had married, had six children, and divorced, that Elias became my grandmother's second husband, in common law. Elias and Victoria had two children, my father Gerald and his younger brother Thomas.

I have lived my life against the backdrop of my ancestors and the histories and events that determined how they would survive and our family continue. Vast in experience and time, in tangibles and intangibles, in a spirituality and presence mysterious and yet so simple, from the other side that is not really another side at all, they move and breathe with me, and I with them.

These places, the places where the ancestors lived—I know they are there, and although I live in different times and I see cars parked, people eating snacks, neon signage, it doesn't bother me because I see the sacredness that is not negated by anything we frail humans might do.

LIFE AMONG THE ITALIANS

ALTHOUGH I AM NOT ITALIAN, I have some lovely Italian childhood memories. Things happen like that here in Onigamiising. The neighborhoods of twentieth-century Duluth have a lot to do with this. Duluth is a city of neighborhoods. Although what comes to mind when thinking of Duluth's immigrant history is predominantly Scandinavians, up to the mid-twentieth century many of Duluth's neighborhoods were made up of extended families from eastern or southern European countries and were distinct in their national cultures. As it has often been in history, some immigrant groups were segregated from the rest of Duluth (this happened earlier with the Scandinavian, Poles, and Jewish people who arrived here after the Scots; history does repeat itself). The Italians were one of those groups.

During the early twentieth century, parts of central Duluth became home to many Italian immigrants who traveled overseas to a new life in America. After the long journey by ship and extensive processing at Ellis Island, some made the train trip to Duluth, particularly the central and near-west hillsides (what we now call Observation Hill). Many settled on the western side of the Point of Rocks, in the scooped-out and blasted-out valley that has been called, over time, Piedmont, Little Italy, Skunk Hollow, Glen Place, and, informally, the Glen. It was at the edge of the Glen that the Anishinaabe man emerged from the rocks after a blasting and walked away, the beginning perhaps of the intertwining story of the Italians and the Anishinaabeg of Onigamiising. Much of the story is incomplete, and much of it has been lost; one day we might know more and understand. *Maagizhaa*; perhaps.

What I remember about Glen Place from when I was a girl in the 1950s and 1960s is that it was just blocks away, a hike over a hump of rock and brush from the Bethel, where my grandfather Elias sometimes lined up for a meal or a bed, and a church service. The Glen got a lot of snow in winter, but during the other three seasons it was lush and green (a little damp, you might say) and overgrown, and unpaved roads were often muddy. The houses were small; a few didn't have plumbing. On the lake side were Superior Street, below Superior Street railroad tracks and factories, and then the Lake Superior harbor. On the other three sides were hills and cliffs of black rock, the massive outcropping that was the Point of Rocks; above that, First Street and the hill. Close by, to the east, was the Bethel, where neighborhood children walked for church events and the annual Christmas party, and men in need walked for a meal and a place to sleep.

The Glen is not large, and as more people moved in and families expanded, the population grew upward—up the hill, that is, above Glen Place, to above the Point of Rocks, up the western and central hillsides to the top of the hill. St. Peter, the Catholic church on Third Street, was built of gabbrous rock, blasted and pried from the Point of Rocks by men who had been stonecutters in Italy. "Little Italy" had outgrown the Glen physically, but the neighborhood feeling was maintained as people moved beyond the little hollow.

My family, the LeGardes, became linked not by blood but by circumstances, including eventually my parents' marriage, to one of the extended Italian families of Onigamiising; we are part of that intertwining of the original Anishinaabeg and the Italians who put such effort into coming to Duluth to give their best shot at the American Dream: a job, perhaps a house, a little vegetable garden, a flock of chickens, some pigs. My first memory of this connection is from the backseat of a car, my dad driving and my grandfather Elias, who was from Fond du Lac, in the passenger seat. We passed the Glen going west on Superior Street; my grandfather mentioned something about a man he knew who lived in the Glen, who had been a cook on one of the ore boats, where my dad had been the cook's helper (fifteen years later my sister married the cook's son—this is the way things happen here in Duluth). Perhaps it was at that time that I first heard the story, just in passing conversation as we drove past the Glen and the Point of Rocks, about the Anishinaabe man who walked out of one of the cracks when the rocks were dynamited, and walked away. Being Anishinaabe, my dad wouldn't have expressed surprise or astonishment; it was something that had happened, unusual things happen, recounting the stories keeps them alive. The words floated to the backseat, where they sprinkled onto me, a little girl, and then germinated, taking root.

How I ended up with an Italian childhood: in the late 1930s my widowed Norwegian grandfather, himself the child of immigrants, bought a house at the top of the Central Hillside and hired the teenaged daughter of a neighboring Italian family, the Iallanardos, to help out with his six children while he worked as a fireman, his shifts being twenty-four hours on and twenty-four hours off, not desirable hours for a combination babysitter and housekeeper. However, this was during the Great Depression and for an eighteen-year-old girl who lived less than a block away and needed to earn some money, it was probably a pretty good job. Within a year they were married. She was thirty when I was born, much younger than other grandmas, and for the rest of her life lived in that same house, close to her parents (who I remember spoke English with the most cheerful and charming of inflections), who lived the rest of their lives in their same house just a block away. Most of her extended family—brothers, sisters, and their children who although not by blood were our cousins—lived nearby. Her name was Carmella; we called her Carmie.

Carmie's family had a shoe repair shop called Pasco's a few blocks down the hill; the building is still there today. Her uncle Pasco, who had come to America as a teenager, employed many of the relatives (by blood and otherwise) to help out over the many decades that the repair shop was in business. Across the street from Carmie and my grandpa was a man who had married a woman from White Earth, whose daughter married my dad's brother Tommy. I believe that Pasco and his brother Sam ("Grandpa Nardo," we called him) thought that Indians were like Italians, in appearance and also in the prejudices they encountered in Duluth. There didn't seem to be much difference to them between their own grandchildren and the mixed-blood kids, like the children across the street and Carmie's step-grandchildren. They loved them all.

Carmie, younger and more stylish than most other grandmas, did much of her housework and cooking in cute ballerina slippers or open-toed high-heeled shoes, with her hair styled (never in curlers that I remember) and lipstick fresh and bright. She had a high, lilting voice that was a delight to hear; when she spoke with her mother they sounded as if they were singing. Grandma Nardo was "old country" although she had been in America since she was a young woman. She wore clean, ironed cotton housedresses and was never without stockings. Her hair was the color of a new nickel, worn in a large donut-shaped bun at the back of her head. She kept a fresh-looking handkerchief tucked into her belt that was more for show than use; she kept a second hanky in her dress pocket, though I never saw her use it. Grandma Nardo was a wonderfully skilled housekeeper who braided rugs and kept pigs and chickens in the fenced yard. She found a use for left-over food and everything else, rarely needing to throw anything away. And both she and Grandpa Nardo were nurturing and kind to my own mother, Patsy, a little girl who lost her own mother when she was three years old. My mother loved helping around the Iallanardo house, loved those

At Carmie's house. From left: my dad, uncle Louie,
Carmie, me, and Aunt Mary.

Italian grandparents, those generous hearts who even called her by an Italian name, Pasqualina.

In the movies, Italian families eat at big crowded tables, laughing and talking a lot; often an older woman is in charge of the kitchen, where her husband does some of the cooking and she gives directions to her grown daughters, who obey quickly and efficiently, and with a flourish. In my own experience that is just the way it was at Carmie's family home up there on top of the hillside in the 1950s and 1960s. The house was small, the kitchen the largest room; the linoleum in the front room, patterned in blues with some pinks to resemble a Persian rug, spotless and shined. In the kitchen, the oilcloth on the table had worn in patterns from people's waists and elbows: scallops at the edges from waists, silver dollars further from the edge, from elbows. Carmie's dad, the grandfather, made the sauce and baked bread, which he took from the oven with his bare hands. Steam rose like fog from the pots and plates of food. Grandma Nardo stood as everyone ate, waving a ladle as though orchestrating the many parts of the conversation and urging everyone to have another helping. She looked quite different from the young woman in the photograph that hung on the wall in the front room: that woman had dark wavy hair dressed in a bouffant and wore a long dress; her waist was incredibly narrow. "Look how little her waist is," I whispered to one of the girl cousins, Terry, as we stood on the shiny, immaculate linoleum in the rather bare front room. We looked through the doorway into the kitchen, at Grandma Nardo's soft, round back in her blue flowered housedress (she almost always wore blue). "They really cinched them in in those days," she whispered back. I saw Terry recently at a high-school graduation party for one of our young relatives (by blood, family, and heart). We had such a lovely, though very short, visit, Terry (called Tootie in those days; I love her childhood nickname) and I, even though we were standing six feet apart and wearing our coronavirus pandemic masks. We are cousins—Terry Italian and French, me Ojibwe, Polish, and Norwegian—because her aunt Carmella married my grandfather Louie (Lauritz).

Carmie's and her parents' houses were at the crest of the hill, on the Skyline and Eleventh Street; just past that were acres and acres of brush and trees, the area rural. Two years after we were born a public-housing project was built right across what had been the little road in front of the Iallanardo grandparents' house; it didn't really change things much except that they no longer kept chickens and pigs in their fenced yard. Between the Iallanardos and Carmie's there was just one house, on the corner. All three are still there today, looking much the same. Each could be seen from the other yards and the families were friendly. It was a year before my parents married that my dad's younger brother, Tommy, married Carol, one of the extended family on the corner, and so my grandpa Elias LeGarde had daughters-in-law from both houses.

And thus our histories and our lives are intertwined, but like any other real story this one is a jigsaw puzzle with a missing box—the pieces eventually fit together, but as the picture emerges, it may not look the way we thought it might. Our families expanded, children grew to adults; many stayed in Duluth, and even in their grandparents' neighborhoods. Some struggled all their lives. Eventually, as young people from immigrant communities married and produced children who were perhaps Italian and Swedish, or Polish and French-Canadian, or Italian and Finnish, and lines between cultures and customs and religions blurred, and prejudices that people felt—"my daughter wants to marry an Italian?"—melted considerably with the birth of a grandchild. But although some children and grandchildren of European immigrants married Indians and had children, the original people of Onigamiising remained apart, separate. Putting it another way I could say that the Indians retained an apartness, a separateness. I don't think this was necessarily because of a lack of acceptance on the part of the non-Indian people of Duluth, although that certainly happened and continues to; there is at the foundation of things a sense of Native identity, and continuity of that identity as a people, that goes far beyond ethnic and cultural pride and survival.

I doubt that I will ever complete the picture puzzle: there are too many pieces that are blurred, sometimes deliberately, in memory or in the recounting of the story. My part in this is very small and limited, and in returning to a child's perspective, it can be comforting. Grandpa Elias, who came and went, whose visits were sometimes awkward occasions because they were so infrequent, was a free spirit unbroken by his life, Carmie the prettiest young grandma around. Grandma Nardo with her nickel-colored hair, who magically wove rugs from rags, brought forth generation after generation of red geraniums that she grew in coffee cans in her enclosed back porch, and came to our house to take care of us when my mother was in the hospital having a baby. Carmie's daughter Mary and her best friend Marie, who as teens, brought out their portable record player and tried to teach us to rock-and-roll, sixty years later still rock-and-roll at weddings. Looking back at all this and watching the puzzle pieces fit in their correct places over the years, I see now that they all knew each other, and knew about each other. About us.

Here is a memory that comes to mind today: a trip downtown on the bus with Carmie. She was wearing cute shoes, of course, this pair with walking heels and bows over the closed toes, and nylon stockings with seams. People dressed nicely to go downtown in those days, and I wore my navy-and-white checked coat, clean anklets, and my new saddle shoes, bought for the first day of school, which wouldn't happen for a couple of weeks but worn that day for the excursion downtown. The sidewalks on Superior Street were filled with people: shoppers, office workers, high-school students hanging out with their friends in front of Woolworth's. Carmie and I went to Glass Block, to Montgomery Ward for a spool of thread, and to the window displays at Wahl's and Gateley's (where my mother had bought my not-yet-to-be-worn first day of school dresses). As we stood waiting for the bus home we chatted. I asked if sometime we could look for a pair of high heels like hers for me, if we saw some in my size. She was open to that. Carmie suddenly said, "Oh, no, look what I did." She opened her hand, and there was the spool of thread. "I forgot to pay for this. We'll have to go back to Ward's." Her mouth pursed slightly; a tiny wrinkle appeared, disappeared, appeared again between her eyebrows. "But we need to get home or Grandpa's supper will be late. . . . Oh, there's the bus."

She took a step, but not toward the bus. "Oh, Grandpa's supper is going to be late," she said regretfully, then took my hand. We walked back to Montgomery Ward, where she apologized to the young lady behind the counter and paid for the thread. Then we went back out onto Superior Street and waited for the next bus.

I don't recall what we had for supper, if Carmie hurried it along or settled on something quick like eggs and oatmeal. My grandpa, who worked hard and was surely looking forward to his supper, would have listened attentively as she recounted our adventures. Perhaps he commented, "Holy Kernumpsky!" (he thought that was a funny thing to say when he was astonished) when she got to the part about finding the spool of thread in her hand. Perhaps, but I don't remember any of that. What I do remember is Carmie making a decision to do the honest thing when nobody would need to know except she herself, and me, a little girl who saw so much that was admirable in Carmie's lipstick, her high heels, and her decision to return to Montgomery Ward to apologize, pay for the thread, and take the later bus.

My cousins, the Italian ones who are cousins by endearment, are all over Duluth; we run into each other often. Mike worked at the UMD coffee shop for quite a while, and my office was right down the hall (this is how things are in Duluth), where sometimes we got a little chatty. "She's my cousin!" he said to the barista, who answered, "Cousins? Really?" in a surprised way. I guess we don't really look alike, but I have always felt that we do, sort of. Mike is very proud of being Italian—he is one of those guys who wears the colors of the Italian flag and loves Facebook memes that start out "You know you're Italian if you . . ."

Mike's mother was Carmie's younger sister, and she, like the rest of the family, never lived far from the Iallanardo house. She was a well-loved lady, and when she died a few years ago, of course we went to her funeral. Sitting on the long bench next to Mike, we talked about the good time we had as kids and how much everybody loved his mother. "They're going to play her favorite song at the end of the service," he said. "What is it?" "Oh, you'll have to wait and see."

It was sweet to sit next to Mike, and his siblings, with several of my brothers and sisters, too, all on the long bench that ran across the room. "It's so nice to see all you LeGardes," he said again. I noticed that there was a lot of dark hair there. "We look like Italians," I said.

Mike paused, a very courteous guy who was obviously thinking that we did not at all, then he nodded his head politely.

The song was "Arrivederci Roma."

THE BEANBAG

When the snow began to thaw, at first we saw
only a trace of flowered calico,
then every day more cotton flowers bloomed,
deep blue blossoms wet with melting snow.
Familiar, it looked. I remembered
forget-me-nots on her favorite housedress
that, when worn out, she crocheted with a hook
into a rug, mostly; the smallest scrap
she sewed into a child's toy, a beanbag.

I remember that dress.
As a child, when she held me close,
my face against her soft, flowered middle
smelling starch and warm geranium
in her soft and cool fleshy embrace
I felt small, an infant, or not yet
born in a cocoon of blue flowered cloth.

Early in spring after she died
one day I recognized that flowered dress:
forget-me-nots on cotton, wet buds of blue flowers
on a beanbag we were kicking around the yard.

Split, it spilled the past

    her kitchen floor
    bumpy patterned linoleum, shiny and bare
    reflecting wavy geraniums in coffee cans,
    nurtured from seeds of their own great-grandmothers

checked oilcloth
leaned to white pearl scallops at the edge
by her daughters' slender, bending waists
and ground to silver dollars, several pairs,
by her ravenous sons' elbows

kitchen woodstove a hot dull black
bread baking in the oven;
above, noodles boiling tomatoes roiling
singing huffs of steam above our heads

I remembered when the beanbag spilled the past;
when it split and spilled the past I remembered,
and picked it up, to see it one more time

and what was that? I looked close, and closer.
Through its frayed weave, in returning to the earth
the bag held life beyond the tiny past.
Split and spilt, its damp side finely pierced
by an infant bean seedling yet blind, but greedy
for the light, born in a cocoon of flowered
blue calico, a pattern wet with snow
forget-me-nots an early sign of spring
entwined now with a trace of tender green.

That dress; I remember her flowered dress.

RAIN, FOG, GHOST, SPIDER

It was the scent of rain that caused me to look up from the reception desk. *He had been watching me from the doorway, too reticent to speak until I looked up and saw him, long-legged and thin, shivering and transparent as sleet.*

"Can I help you?"

"Are you Linda LeGarde?" *He had used my maiden name.*

In May 1999, the day after my aunt Janice died and a few days before the final defense of my dissertation, a Native man walked in the rain from downtown to the Student Affairs office in the College of Education and Human Service Professions at the University of Minnesota Duluth, where I worked, several miles and almost all uphill, into the foreign and alien world of higher education. Once inside, he would have wandered the long, interconnected hallways of UMD without asking directions until he came upon Bohannon Hall, in his humility expecting no acknowledgment of his existence from the students. Almost all of them white, middle-class, and absorbed in their own youth, they would have given to this rain-soaked, frail, and (to them) foreign Native man with the long, dampened hair, many years their elder, plenty of room to walk. I am certain that no one asked if he needed directions or offered help; his presence was so different from what they were used to that perhaps they were unable to recognize that he was even there. Perhaps, if anyone noticed him at all they thought he was a ghost; he walked almost as invisibly as one.

I smelled rain, sensed movement from a presence in the doorway, transparent as sleet. Beads of fog in his thin gray hair and on the shoulders of his jacket caught and blurred the overhead glare from the fluorescent ceiling lights as he stood in the doorway. "Can I help you?" I asked. ("Are you really there?" I thought.)

Leaning lightly against the doorway for balance, he shivered, coughed; the hand that came out of his pocket to cover the cough was chapped and deep lavender in color. Apologetically, he wiped the hand on his sleeve and took a step into the room; he cleared his throat, crossed his arms, swayed. Would he fall? I wondered. Then he looked directly at me, a connection so unusual in Native men of his generation, and uncrossed his thin arms. In the fog of fluorescent light over the weather he had brought indoors, he might have been shape-shifting into a spider; he might have been preparing to weave his words into the story that was to come. But I didn't know that yet. Was he lost?

He asked if I was Linda LeGarde.

He had used my maiden name.

What determines the intersections of lives? We Ojibwe believe that all that happens was meant to be, our unknown destinies long ago seen and predetermined by the Creator. This is a matter of faith with or without a labored convolution of human-limited reasoning; how else can this particular late-afternoon interlude be explained? I was nearing the end of my fourteenth year working in that office, managing student records and processing their teaching license applications. During those years as full-time office worker and all-time mother, I had completed a bachelor's degree and then a master's; with the defense of my research and the submission of my dissertation, my doctoral course work and research would be complete, as far as the University of Minnesota was concerned. But not my education.

He introduced himself and told me that he had come to find me because he had heard that I was recording Indian boarding school history; he was there to honor me for that, he said, holding out and then opening a folded and tied package of horsehair and leather. Spread across one palm, the package became a pair of ladies' dance ornaments, each crimped with a piece of tin that shone as softly as an old dime. My hands opened like a chalice to accept the smoky-scented gift that was still warm and a little damp from rain, perspiration, and, I would come to realize, his weeping heart. He had made these for me, he said, because I had honored our people by caring for our stories. Would I like to hear his story? he asked.

I have known men like him all of my life, modest American Indian warriors who walk in humility and faith toward the destinations at which they are meant to arrive.

"It will be an honor to hear you speak," I said, with the formality that is part of Ojibwe courtesy in situations of profound gravity. Ordinarily, common Ojibwe manners and hospitality might have meant that once we had said hello I would have offered him a chair, offered him coffee, asked where he was from and who his family was; he would have replied and asked me the same. We would have eventually come to a commonality of people and relationships by blood or experiences. This conversation, although politely unhurried, proceeded around those cultural shibboleths with an undercurrent of urgency that trumped social custom.

He half-unzipped his jacket and took from an inside breast pocket a small rolled-up stack of papers, then sat but did not remove his jacket, although the shoulders were wet from rain. "I'd like for you to see these," he said in that unhurried and urgent way. "These are some articles, and some things I have written down, about when I was in a residential school in Canada. I want to tell you about it."

My research, a series of sixteen interviews with American Indian people, primarily Ojibwe, with individual or family connections to boarding schools in the upper Midwest, had been completed months earlier. The fourth chapter, which was the interpretation of the data, had been written; the fifth and final chapter, which was the summary of the research project, was in final draft form, nearly ready for submission to my committee. "Why today?" I prayed silently. "My aunt has died; a rescheduling of my research defense will delay the awarding of my degree; my family needs me; my soul and spirit, my hours, are filled to capacity. Why today, why this afternoon?"

The answer was that there are times when a person must stop thinking and only watch, listen, and breathe.

"Here is an article about the priest at the school in Canada I went to. I was just a little boy when I went there . . . ," he began.

In America, the dismantling of the Indian boarding school system began in the mid-1930s, a process that took decades; we descendants of the boarding school generations continue to experience the rupturing effects on individuals, families, and communities every day. In Canada, the Indian boarding school experience is historically even closer: the dismantling did not begin until the 1970s, which means that the trauma is very close and recent to people who are still living. Those interviewed for my research had gone to Indian boarding schools in the United States during the 1920s to 1960s or were descendants of the children who had attended during those decades. The man in the doorway was a boarding school child in Canada during the 1960s and 1970s, which meant that he was probably no more than fifty years old; he looked much older than that.

He seemed very tired, this man who walked several miles in the rain, almost all uphill, yet he spoke for nearly an hour. He paused occasionally, not because he expected a reply or reaction from me but to think or to take a deeper breath before continuing his story. I listened, listened, breathing with his slow rhythm, inhaling the story and the lucidity of alcohol from his breath, his clothing, and perspiration.

How I would have liked to close the door to the office in order to not interrupt his story for the questions, requests, and demands that had become my daylight hours over the past decade and a half (financial holds on registration, arguments and tears over academic probation status, teacher licenses slow in coming from the State of Minnesota, the short supply of toilet paper in the women's bathroom across the hall). But miraculously, not a single student or professor came into Student Affairs for help or with a question during that time. Surely the occasion must have been, as the old Ojibwe used to say and still do, meant to be.

He held the newspaper clippings in one hand, occasionally setting them on one knee and rereading, touching the print with his fingertips as he interacted with the reporter's story and his own by touching the tangibles of paper and written words. He told me that there was much more to the priest's story as well as his own, more than a reporter could have written. His own spirit crushed and damaged but not yet destroyed, he spoke so very personally about the pain he lived with, and the effort it took for him to live day to day with memories that lived in him. "This is something that people need to know about," he said. "This is what was done to me," and he began to weep; that is, his eyes wept steady tears while his voice remained even and his movements, slight gestures made by fine-boned hands and frail arms, remained as contained as they would at the window of a confessional. Once or twice he tapped his foot for several seconds; aware, he stopped as though hearing someone from decades ago directing him to not fidget. Again and again his eyes shone as they filled, dulled as they emptied, while he talked, giving me words that I could only hear from a past only he could see. Occasionally our eyes met, in repeat of that unusual circumstance for Ojibwe conversations, but, again, urgency overriding conventions, we did not have much time.

After a while he paused and asked if I would do him the biggest favor. I replied that I would. Could I please call detox for him, he asked, and took a piece of paper from his pocket with the telephone number written down. I did that. They had been expecting his call, they said; he could come anytime. He rose to leave; I offered him a ride back downtown.

He was, like so many Anishinaabe men I know, courteous to the point of courtliness. At the door to the parking lot, he offered me his jacket because I wasn't wearing a coat. He was shivering again, I noticed, and declined. As we walked in the rain to my car, we were silent, and all the way down the hill, but as we got closer to the hospital he began to comment on the rain, the windshield wipers, how heavy the traffic was. Small talk.

He was frightened, I thought. "Are you nervous?" I asked.

"A little. I'm OK."

"It will be all right." I didn't know that, but I began to chatter lamely about courage, and finding strength inside one's self, and about survival, and about the future, that things could get better. Words, just words; what could I tell him that he didn't already know? He nodded politely. "Mm hmm," he affirmed each thing I said, in the mannerly way of the Ojibwe. Then he said, after I parked the car in front of detox, "So, you want to go get a drink? E-e-ey, just kidding!" and so we were laughing as we walked up the wet sidewalk and through the glass doors.

Detox was pretty quiet; nobody was in the waiting room, and a woman at the registration window told us to come right up to the window. "Are you together?" she asked, as pleasantly as if we were dinner patrons at a nice restaurant, and she the hostess.

We answered at the same time, he "Yes" and me "I'm his ride." I stood next to him but far enough away to give him some privacy, which distanced us: his voice changed as he spoke to the woman at the window, sounding less frightened and even somewhat relieved and trusting. His paperwork complete, the woman told him that she was going to let him inside. Opening a door, she said, "You can say good bye for now."

He nodded at me, at last and heartbreakingly dry-eyed, and followed the woman. Before he went through the door to detox, he told me that he would like to write his story someday.

That night I rewrote my final chapter, the summary of conclusions that were not really conclusions at all. Two days later, I left the after-funeral lunch in the Lutheran church basement to head to UMD to defend my dissertation. Before I started, I mentioned to the examining committee that I had just come from my aunt's funeral. They seemed a little surprised, yet relieved that they had not had to reschedule the defense, especially the members who had driven to Duluth from Minneapolis.

"Is everyone ready to begin? Tell us about your research project; tell us what you learned," the committee chair requested.

I looked past the five men sitting at the conference table to the sixteen people who had given me their time, their stories, and a part of their lives, and to the rainy afternoon visitor, the apparition who might at that moment be eating a hot meal in a warm room at detox, the man who had by grace of the Creator become the reality of Chapter 5: Summary.

"I've learned that there is not as much difference as I thought between the tangible and the intangible," I began.

The man who was as transparent as sleet and I spoke just once again, on a sunny day a year or so later when he again ventured back to UMD to see me. This time he was on his way to Canada, and not sure when he would be back. He left with me an envelope with some notes that he had written down about an old Ojibwe story, the comforting one about the spider and the baby that appealed to the man whose own need for comfort and nurturing had been betrayed by a priest, a system, a government, the twentieth century.

I think that he would have liked to have been the spider who comforted the baby and wove the magical web of protection that separated bad dreams from the sweet blessings of the good. *Maagizhaa*, for all we know, in an earlier life perhaps he was. *Maagizhaa*. That is a perhaps, a maybe, a wish. A possibility and hope.

"Would you hold on to these for a while?" he asked, "and could I ask you to do another favor for me, too? It's something I forgot to take care of." He had a claim ticket for a pair of binoculars that he had left at a pawnshop. "Sometime when you're downtown, do you think you could redeem them and send them to a friend of mine? I'll give you the money to get them out and send them."

"Sure, I'd be glad to do that. I have to go down to CAIR to pick up my uncle's pills in a couple of days, anyway." CAIR was the Center for American Indian Resources, in the old Catholic Diocese of Duluth building, where the Indian Health Services clinic was.

He handed me the ticket. "Do you know where it is?"

I knew where the pawnshop was. The building was the former Union Gospel Mission, where my grandfather, a boarding school child himself, had as a grown man visited many times for a sermon and a meal, and hoping for a bed, as had hundreds of American Indian apparitions over the years. The mission had moved across the street years before, but the words "Union Gospel Mission" painted on the original, century-old building in letters six feet high, were still visible to everyone on the east side of the building. I thought of my grandfather every time I saw them.

"Sure; I know where it is." I took the ticket with my left hand, the same hand with which we accept tobacco, the hand closest to the heart.

"Can I borrow a pen and a piece of paper? I'll write down the address." His writing was spidery and elegant, like my grandfather's. "One more thing. . . . Will you just put a note in with the binoculars? Just write 'Compliments of Artelle.'" He gave me a handful of bills. "I think this will cover it."

I didn't see Artelle again. Two years later, I saw his name in another newspaper story about child abuse in Canadian residential schools during the 1960s written by a reform-minded reporter who I uncharitably thought added another layer to the exploitations of generations of Indian children by sensationalizing the story for his own and his employer's gain. I don't know if Artelle ever got a chance to write his own story; I haven't come across it, but I hope that he did. For many reasons: for history, for the Indians, for those generations that will come after his and mine, for himself.

I did get to the pawnshop, as I had said I would. Although I had walked past the Union Gospel Mission building countless times and glanced into the window when I was a young woman, I had never been inside. It had changed, of course, in the years since my grandfather listened to a sermon in return for a meal and a bed. The semi-sheer white curtains that used to hang on the bottom half of the large windows on either side of the door had been removed; the rows of folding chairs and the small lectern used for sermons were gone. The room was half the size that I remembered; it had been partitioned off and Sheetrocked. In the middle of the new wall was a doorway, in front of the door a store counter that displayed watches, jewelry, several cameras, and a video recorder in its locked glass case. Nothing in the case looked to be of great monetary value; who has anything of value to pawn in that rough section of east First Street in Duluth?

Five feet into the shop an electronic "ding" chimed; a man emerged from the back. He looked me over quickly, as he would anyone who walked through the door. Did this woman in her office outfit, a khaki skirt, cardigan, and cotton blouse, want to pawn something? Was she lost and in need of direction (I was, but not in the way he probably thought). "Can I help you?" he asked.

"Can I retrieve a pair of binoculars if it's not my own ticket?" I dug in the inside pocket of my neat and functional purse, found the folded pawn ticket and handful of bills.

"As long as you've got the ticket, sure. Be right back," he said. It took him a minute to find the binoculars in the back room, a minute more to take the money and exchange the tickets, one paid for and one redeemed. During this I looked around, but my grandfather did not make an appearance, nor was he on the sidewalk outside when I left.

I mailed the binoculars, slipping inside the case a Post-it note on which I wrote, "Compliments of Artelle." Not long after that, Artelle's friend sent me a note of thanks for the binoculars and for being so kind as to send them.

Artelle's draft of the story about the spider who comforts a lonely baby in need of nurturing is in a box of things that I have saved for when we meet again, an occasion that may or may not come during my lifetime.

What prayers might be said for a grieving and prematurely old apparition who walks miles in the rain to honor someone who has not yet earned it? My prayers for Artelle were that he would recover and lead a good life; that he would overcome the demons that should never have been his and that sat on his shoulders as they sat on my grandfather's, on mine, and on the shoulders of every Native person that I have ever known; that when he left detox he would throw those demons down onto the concrete sidewalk where people would walk on and over them until finally they wore to a mere trace of shadow on the porosity of mortar; that it would rain and snow on that shadow until, weather-battered and broken, the sun bleached and vaporized it to nothing.

As we look for answers to our prayers, we endeavor endlessly to achieve levels of faith and patience that are beyond our human capacity. Still, we look for signs. Could this be one? we wonder, knowing in our hearts our limitations. Blind and deaf yet seeking, we can't always necessarily see or understand what is truth and what is our yearning to know. That rainy afternoon of darkness and light, as real today as it was then, that tangibly and intangibly seen and touched manifestation of the patterns and mysteries of a much larger story of which we are a part, was that an answer? I wonder today as I wondered yesterday, and the day before, and as I will tomorrow.

PART II
GICHIGAMI
HEARTS

WAAWAASHKESHI

MY UNCLE BOB DROUILLARD was born in 1912 in Chippewa City, a settlement of Ojibwe people a mile and a half northeast of Grand Marais, on the shores of Lake Superior. Uncle Bob lived to be a very old man, and though he didn't talk a lot he was pleased to be asked about his life experiences as a little boy in Chippewa City, a combat Marine in the Pacific Theater, an underwater welder on oil rigs, and sometimes his days in the Indian boarding schools he had attended. I loved listening to him. The last person in our family fluent in the Ojibwe language from childhood, Uncle Bob was kind and patient in letting me try to converse with him. He was thoughtful in his attempts to ask me questions that would be easy to understand and answer. In trying to understand me he would sometimes look a little puzzled, and I would laugh, embarrassed; he responded every time, "No . . . no . . . You're doing good, keep it up." Once he said, "You sound like my grandma," and I pictured him as a little boy in Chippewa City, there at the shoreline helping his grandmother as he learned how to do everyday tasks of life in those days, her spoken instructions in Ojibwemowin, the language, and her example in the way she approached the tasks themselves, as humble, thankful, and considerate *mindemooye* Nokomis and matriarch.

To live on the shore of Lake Superior is to live with orientation to water, sky, and forest. Standing on the rocks at the shoreline, hundreds of miles of forest are at one's back, the vastness of Gichigami at the front; the sky and water meet at the horizon, ever more elusive to anyone traveling toward it. We see that same horizon today from Duluth and all the way up the North Shore of Gichigami, horizon to the east and land to the west, water and sky meeting in that elusive, ever more distant beauty that it always has. George Morrison, the Ojibwe painter of the Grand Portage band, integrated the Lake Superior horizon into much of his work; when I look at his paintings and sculptures, I am aware of the balance and symmetry of water and sky, physical and natural worlds. Morrison, who was born in Chippewa City, was a lifelong friend of my uncle Albert, Bob's younger brother. Albert and

George attended the Indian boarding school in Hayward, Wisconsin, a sad and terrible place in Albert's memories, with a sadistic—Albert's word—staff. Their lives took different directions after school, but George returned to the North Shore after he retired, and Albert visited him every few years when he traveled to Duluth to see family here and up to Grand Portage Reservation, thirty miles farther up the shore from their boyhood home, for the August powwow.

The Chippewa City community lived with an ever-present awareness of the natural world around them interwoven with the spirituality that is inseparable to all made by the Creator, including human beings; the Ojibwe teachings of gratitude for everything in existence certainly included the integrated beauties and challenges of that place. This was part of everyday life, how people lived.

When Bob was a small boy, he spent most of his time with his grand-mother, who lived right on the lake, helping her with chores like chopping wood, fetching water, and snaring rabbits for their meat and their fur. Bob's grandmother didn't speak English, and so Ojibwemowin was the language spoken in their home; my uncle was one of that generation of Ojibwe whose worldview, speech patterns, and interaction with everything around them was rooted in how things were regarded and expressed in the Ojibwe language of days that were very different from now.

Traditional Ojibwe knowledge and worldview are naturally integrated with the actions of everyday existence; as Bob put it, they lived like the old-time Indians. The community—fourteen families at the Chippewa City settlement at the time, all Indian, many related in some way—depended on each other for both subsistence and spiritual support. They riced in late summer and maple-sugared in the spring, helping their neighbors out where help was needed. The men worked for pay in the woods sometimes, as lum-berjacks, and they hunted and snared; when the men were away, the women had to take care of things at home, which was hard work. Children were part of the work, included and taught from the time they were small, and they were proud of being able to contribute to the community; that was the way that Ojibwe families had raised their young for generations. Bob explained to me that the people didn't refer to those tasks as work, that the word *work* was used for doing things for pay for someone else, like the timber companies. What we might think of today as work around the house and neighborhood was also a lot of fun; the concept of work as a means of keeping food, shel-ter, and company also involved what we might think of today as play.

Bob started school in Grand Marais at the regular public school, where in the early grades the children from Chippewa City were in the same room as the other children, many of whose parents were Norwegian immigrants. He had a photograph of the "school bus" made by one of the Norwegian farmers to get the children transported to Grand Marais during winter: it consisted of a wooden box on sled runners, with a small door at the back and a square cut out in the front, probably about 8 x 8 inches, for the driver to see out. Inside were a benches on each side where the students would sit, probably four on each side. The box was just tall enough for the driver to sit or kneel. I asked if it was cold inside the bus. No, he didn't remember feeling cold, Bob answered. The Norwegian farmer sometimes brought in a metal box with hot coals or smoldering wood inside; he was a nice guy, and they had a good time.

On the lovely summer afternoon of this conversation with Bob, he paused, then, thinking. "And then when I got to be eight years old, it was time for me to go away from home to Indian school. I was the oldest in my family and I felt that my grandmother needed me, so it was hard to leave. That last summer seemed to go by really fast. I do particularly remember a day there at Chippewa City from the last summer before I went away to school—a nice day, sunny out and the lake was sparkling. You know how it is a pretty dark blue on days like this, with sun sparkles on the waves?" He looked past me, past the houseplants that sat on the table in front of the door to the deck at my dad's house, looking for Lake Superior two miles down the hill but obscured by trees and Duluth, and for the Lake Superior at the edge of Chippewa City, unobscured and real as it had been in 1920.

Eight-year-old Bob was by himself on the shore, walking around and skipping rocks. The waves were small, lapping in one after another against the large black rocks; pebbles clicked and rattled as they were pushed against the rocks and then away back into the water as the waves receded. Next to the largest rock, sheltered from the wind and high enough to keep it from washing away in the tide, was a rowboat, turned on its side. Bob walked around the boat—the people kept it in nice condition for ricing and fishing and going places—and then sat on one of the large black rocks, listening to the waves and rattling pebbles as he watched the lake, the sun sparkling on the rippling, lapping water. The music of the lake and feel of sun-warmed stone against his body was soothing, like being rocked and sung to, and Bob almost fell asleep.

"Then, all of a sudden there was a crashing sound from the woods. I looked up and out from the woods ran a deer, straight past the rock where I was sitting and right into the water, its legs thrashing and churning the water as it began to swim. From the woods there was still the sound of crashing through brush, and I wondered if there were more deer, and then two men run out; I knew both, my uncle and our neighbor Antoine, and they were chasing the deer. They yelled to me, 'Into the boat! Antoine shot him, and he is hit!' I run, and pull the boat to push off to the water, and all three of us get in, Antoine rowing like crazy and my uncle unwinding a rope from the bottom of the boat. We're getting closer to the buck and he is tiring, he is hurt and the men had to make it quick. My uncle swung the rope around his neck and Antoine shot him. We towed him back to the shore, and they butchered him right there, me making myself useful where I could; I was only eight, pretty small yet. As they divided the meat, people from the four-teen families came to the shore and everyone took some home; that was the custom in those days, when someone got a deer, then the fourteen families shared. The custom was that old people, or people who were sick, got the best parts; we were proud to be able to give the best of the deer to them.

"I felt like a man, like my uncle and Antoine. It was a day that I have never forgotten, bringing deer meat to the families, and that memory has stayed with me for eighty years. Not too long after that, it was time to go; I had to go away from home, from my grandma and from Chippewa City, to Indian school. At boarding school, I was a boy; I sure hoped that I could go home to Chippewa City sometime, where I could be with the men and do the things that men did. That was a long time ago, Indians living like that. Those days were good ones, and I sure have good memories of living at Chippewa City, right there on the lake."

Uncle Bob lifted his cup of tea from the table next to the couch, but instead of sipping looked over the cup and through the dining-room window. To his back was the kitchen, outside the kitchen window the hill that sloped down to the Point of Rocks, Goat Hill, and the West End, where he lived as a young man in a family of many branches, twigs, and tendrils that grew and spread across the country but always cared for and nourished its roots. He was looking at all that, I think.

Outside, the overgrown lilac bushes had bloomed weeks before; the leaves, dense in the late-summer dampness of the front yard and taller than the window, were a wall of deep green as lush, I thought, as the woods back of Chippewa City when Uncle Bob was eight years old.

MOOZ

THIS IS A STORY I have heard only once, decades ago. It is from the northern lakeshore of Gichigami, its origin in the days of treaty making, during the upheavals of lands lost and people relocated, those days of defeat and survival, of families fragmenting under the duress of the times. As the story goes, one man became separated from the Anishinaabeg of his tribe. Whether this was by choice or other circumstance we don't know; everyone has a story that is part of the larger web of stories that is our existence. Perhaps he had fallen behind the others who were walking westward toward what would be their reservation lands; perhaps he decided that the westward walk was too much like the route taken to the next world by Anishinaabeg who had died; or perhaps he was simply lost. He carried his gun, and on his back a blanket that held some tools—a hatchet, perhaps a hunting knife, a tin cup, some dried meat, fat, and berries—a good Ojibwe man of those days would know how to make use of those things, to conserve and to have a knowledge of the gifts placed on the earth for our subsistence by the Creator.

In Ojibwe language the word *ingo* indicates a single unit (for example, the number 6 is *ingo-dwaaswi,* one unit added to the base group, which is 5). *Ingo* is sometimes a nickname, too, that is given in childhood and can be carried through adulthood. It is a name, one of several, that my nephew Michael was called by when he was little. I have always thought of the man in this story as having that name—it suits him, I believe. Beyond that it is enough to say that alone, he made a life for himself that, though solitary, was satisfying.

He built a small birchbark hut as Nokomis had when she fell from the moon to the earth, and began the life of a solitary person who relied on himself to build, gather, hunt, fish, and cook. Industrious, his time filled with the work of survival and in the company of his own thoughts, he was never idle or lonely; content, if he had pondered such a thing, he might have wondered how a man would have time in his life for interactions with other people.

The way I heard the story, a light snow fell during a late fall night and had cleared by morning, leaving just enough snow that when he stepped outside, Ingo saw the tracks immediately. "A moose," he said to himself. "Not a large one, probably young enough for the meat to be tender, and small enough for ease in butchering; a nice size that might very well be enough, pieced out with rabbit meat, to last one man for most of the winter."

He took his gun and followed the tracks, which led to the large black rocks on the shore of Gichigami and disappeared. "Weweni," he muttered, climbing over the icy sharpness to the edge of the lakeshore, where the rocks were much smaller and smoother, black pebbles that over centuries had broken off as the waves, strongest in late fall storms, shattered the weakest points of the rocks, pulling the pieces into the water and then tossing them against each other again and again. He walked along the water's edge on those slippery pebbles thinking how soon the lake would freeze over and he would be able to walk on the ice, taking a shortcut across the inlet and the large outcropping of rock just up ahead—then he saw movement, a dark form near the top of the outcropping. Moving quickly and silently in wet moccasins over the pebbles, he got close enough to take aim; he raised his gun and looked down the barrel at the moose who, sensing his presence, turned to look behind her—and she was not a moose at all, but a young woman with long dark hair and large, sad, purple eyes.

In shock, relief, and anger, Ingo asked the woman what she was doing there; she didn't answer, but walked slowly toward him. She was thin, he saw, large-boned and awkward, homely and pathetic in her ragged dress, cold and barefoot. And she followed him home, a fine board house he had built to suit himself, every piece of it just as he liked, where he allowed her to sleep on a pile of furs by the fire.

The smell of maple sugar and frying meat woke him the next morning; she had hauled and heated water, made hot maple tea from the previous spring's sugar harvest, and fried several pieces of rabbit from the sack of meat he kept hanging from a tree not far from the house. This irritated him—was she trying to insinuate herself into his existence, eat his food, live in his house? He told her that she could stay another day, but only if she made herself useful, and left to check his snares.

The next morning, Ingo woke to the sound of wind; outside, snow was blowing into drifts that unevenly covered the yard outside the house. Inside, the woman sat mending the hole in an old pair of deerskin leggings. On the cookstove a pot boiled; the scent of cooking potatoes mingled with that of steaming raspberry tea. The woman spoke her first words: "Miijim temigad adopowining." The food is on the table. This again irritated Ingo—

she had certainly felt free to dig around in the food he had worked so hard to harvest and store for the winter, and now here he was feeding two; however, he couldn't tell her to leave today, he said to himself, not in a storm like that.

Two nights became three, and four, and more as the cold and snow of winter progressed and the woman continued to make herself useful, as Ingo had instructed her to do. She was thrifty, he noticed, a skilled cook who never wasted a scrap. She set snares that caught rabbits cleanly; she dressed the meat cleanly, saving the bones for household tools and the soft pelts for winter caps, linings for moccasins; she cut strips of the lightest pelts and began weaving them into a blanket. Ingo muttered under his breath that once it was finished, she could move back to her old place by the fire from the bed that they had come to share—at the time he had told himself that the nights were so cold and she was so skinny, the last thing he needed was for her to sicken from lack of warmth. He told himself that when the weather warmed up in the spring, he would tell her to take the rabbit-skin blanket with her when she left.

"If you've got time to spend on a fancy blanket, you've got time to help haul that other meat stash from that stand of jack pines up the shore tomorrow," he said.

On the return trip, she stumbled over a tree root hidden under the ice-crusted snow and fell onto her hands and knees, dropping the sack of frozen meat, which skittered across the ice. Silently and cautiously, she tried to rise on the slippery surface.

"How clumsy she is," Ingo thought to himself as he took hold of her waist and arm and pulled to her feet. "Weweni," he said. The expression in her purple eyes was appreciative and, suddenly to Ingo, mesmerizing. "Jiibik," he thought to himself. "Is she trying to make magic?" The woman lowered her eyes, Ingo shook his head and looked away, the spell broken. "Weweni," he repeated in a rough voice. "Be careful."

The story may be predictable, but that can be comforting. The young woman, industrious and skilled in the ways of living in the woods and on the lakeshore, created a life of companionship and ease that was new to Ingo: she fished, trapped, kept the cabin tidy and his clothes repaired, and generally made herself useful. She moved wild rosebushes from the woods to the cabin door, one on each side, and looked to Ingo whenever she thought he was not looking at her, which was most of the time. Grudgingly, he tolerated this from the pitiful creature who had intruded into his life. And one evening as she stitched new soles to the vamps of his worn moccasins, humming in a low voice, he noticed that her dark hair was shiny and thick, and of the same purple tinge as her eyes, that the boniness of her arms was oddly, pleasingly graceful, that her dress, cleaned and repaired, draped in interesting ways over her lap and her knees. Below the scallops of the skirt her ankles were slender, her large feet that she tapped occasionally to her tuneless humming strong-looking in tight moccasins.

From the corner of his eye, Ingo watched her silently as she shaped a rabbit skin to the inside of each moccasin.

What is probably predictable is that she gave birth to a baby the following spring, and for several springs after; that their children grew to adulthood and began their own families; that they prospered, and that as settlers moved in, they were hospitable and generous with their material goods, their hearts and spirits. That Ingo treated his wife with honor and respect, and that as the couple aged, they were cared and provided for by their large extended family.

There is in Anishinaabe elderhood a wisdom and kindness that has been learned and tempered over the years. With this comes a gratitude for what one has been given in life, sadness that this cannot go on forever, and a sense of obligation to educate and prepare the generations that will follow in order that Anishinaabe ways will continue. The story of Ingo and his wife ends as stories about elders must end, with a departure. When the wife of many years passed to the next life, she was mourned by the many who loved her—children, grandchildren, friends, and neighbors, people she had helped and taught by example. Some traveled from town to the house, which was no longer by itself but surrounded by the homes of the shoreline village that had grown up near and around it. Some brought food: cakes, cooked wild rice, lugalette. The family received everyone as welcome guests, just as she would have in her shy way. On the fourth day, her body was carried by her grandsons out to the woods, where she was buried, her grave marked, but only temporarily, as was the custom, with a stick pushed into the ground. Back at the house, her daughters sorted through her possessions that would be given to those who would use and honor them: her plaid wool shawl to her oldest daughter, her sewing box to a daughter-in-law, her favorite maple sugar candy mold to a grandson. In the evening, everyone went back to their own homes—"We'll be back tomorrow with some wood," said one of the sons—and Ingo was again *ingo*, alone.

In the morning, the old widower woke early, to a house that was very clean and very quiet. Putting a pot of coffee on the stove to boil, he noticed that his wife's moccasins were next to his, on the mat just inside the back door as always. Sorrow and comfort pressed tenderly on the bruise that was his heart as he bent to put his own moccasins on his old feet.

"Ai," he said softly. "Ai." He poured a cup of coffee and stepped outside. "Nice day out," he addressed the sky. "Miigwech."

Ingo walked, an old widower's slow walk, down the path from the house toward the lake, where the sun was a half circle of orange moving almost discernibly up from the blue-gray morning horizon. Along the shoreline, he zigzagged a little as small waves moved up over the pebbles, smooth under his moccasins as he rounded the inlet. He stopped at the bluff, wondering if he should try to climb it, and saw a shadow move against the rock, a young woman perhaps, tall and thin, with long dark hair. He held his breath as she stepped out into the sun, and it was not her at all but a young cow moose who looked back at him with purple eyes and then turned around and walked away from the lakeshore and into the woods.

LAKE HEARTS

ALONG THE NORTHERN SHORE of Lake Superior are many rock outcroppings and water inlets. For the thousands of years since the glacier stopped in its movement south and melted, waves have washed small rocks and driftwood onto the shores of the inlets, worn and smoothed the smaller outcroppings down, and dashed themselves against the higher, pine-topped outcroppings.

Martin Drouillard, my grandmother Victoria's first husband, was born in Chippewa City. Martin and Victoria met at the Vermilion Lake Indian School, across Lake Vermilion from Tower, Minnesota, where they were students, and after they finished school, paid workers. When they married, they moved to Chippewa City, where their six children were born. After a house fire, around 1920, they decided to move down the shore to Duluth. Both still spent quite a bit of time—even after they parted sometime in the late 1920s—living at or in extended visits to Chippewa City, Grand Marais, and Grand Portage Reservation—where, a mile or so inland from the lake, Martin built a cabin and tourist stand at the side of Old Highway 61, in those days the road to Canada. Martin and Victoria remained on friendly terms, generally: the Drouillard children and, later, the LeGarde children (of my grandfather Elias LeGarde, Vicky's second husband) often visited and stayed at the tourist stand as well as with friends and relatives in Grand Portage. The trip up and down the shore had a number of challenges in those days: the road was completed in the late 1920s but still followed the many hills and dips of the terrain along the lakeshore, like a natural roller coaster. The trip took two days, as Uncle Albert recalled; it was exhausting for the adults, and since few people had cars, those that did took as many people along as could fit. Albert had better memories of taking the steamer. It was too expensive to do more than a few times, but very exciting to move so quickly through water, the ship plowing against the waves, out far enough to avoid reefs and rocks under the surface. The lake is formidable and can turn choppy and dangerous very quickly. Albert loved telling me about a trip once from Grand Marais to Duluth in weather that became stormy, with high winds and waves. The passengers and crew were not only frightened but seasick, everyone except for the captain and Albert, who was perhaps ten years old. He stood by the captain during the trip and enjoyed himself very much. In his later years—and he lived to be an old man—he visited Grand Portage to attend the Rendezvous Powwow every August that he could, driving up the new Highway 61 that had been rerouted to follow the lakeshore directly to Grand Portage, commenting to me every time how smooth and straightened-out the road was.

One August evening, when he stopped in Duluth on his way back home from the powwow, Albert and I went to Barnes & Noble for coffee. He found a book of Lake Superior ships and showed me the steamer he had been on during the storm when he was a boy. "It's a nice drive from Grand Portage, took not much over three hours; not like the old days, or on the steamer," he said, more to himself than to me. "The weather . . . you could never really predict it, still can't. It's a big lake, and there's a lot underneath, below the surface, even when the waves are small. There's a lot there that we don't see."

Highway 61 is, as Albert said, a lovely drive along the lakeshore, sometimes thrillingly close to the water. I recall my husband and me driving one night from the Gunflint Lodge (how I loved seeing Justine Kerfoot's cabin home there) in the Boundary Waters to Grand Marais, and on down to Duluth just ahead of a major April snowstorm that blew in oddly and unusually from the southwest, stranding people who would leave Grand Marais the next morning. The lake was so high that night and moved strangely, not in waves so much as rolling water; the wind was sometimes directionless, sometimes coming from many directions and the moon was still out, lighting the snow at each side of the road before the clouds moved in. We watched the road intently, knowing that as we approached any curve, water might be covering the road and we would have to turn around and go back north, which we knew would be even more dangerous in that weather. We were relieved to get back to Duluth—taking that risky night drive was probably not a wise decision and we were exhilarated at having won a bet with nature and time—and told ourselves to remember to not try that again.

In the back of my mind, but present there just the same all during the drive and after we arrived home, were Albert's words about what is under the surface of the lake that we don't see.

LAKE SPIRITS

WE ONLY KNOW about the mishibizhiig, the underwater spirit beings in the lake, by oral tradition and some of the very old recountings by way of the wintertime stories or on the sacred scrolls, or on a rare, very old pictograph in places that only Ojibwe spiritual leaders know about and can access.

The mishibizhiig live in the water, far below the surface, and have never been seen by a human being, except for one. Created by the Creator for reason and purpose, they have been placed in a world that is underwater, just as we above the surface have been created for reason and purpose determined by the Creator and placed in our world above water.

This story is from a long time ago, and I don't remember the first time I heard it or where I was. This is a lake story that is true, that has no specific names, dates, or places—and any of it that is difficult to understand is also true. We were not created to understand and to know everything or to pursue understanding and knowledge zealously and excessively; these will come to us if that is meant to be, and if that is not meant to be, a good Anishinaabe will accept it with gratitude, humility, and grace. The story is its own truth.

It is not that long ago that in a settlement there lived a woman who was distinctive in that her hair had turned white suddenly when she was still young. She was quiet, a reticent person who didn't speak much but kept her own counsel, living a good, industrious life taking care of her family—her husband, children, parents, grandparents, aunties, uncles, cousins—the extended Ojibwe family of the times that still continues today, although perhaps in different forms. She went about her daily tasks in her quiet way, fine filaments of hair that worked itself from her braid catching sunlight and cloudshine, waving like small dancers during the day, those same filaments capturing moonlight and dancing with the stars overhead at night.

"There's no hiding with that hair," a neighbor commented to her sister. "You can see her wherever she is."

"It is whiter than her grandfather's," replied the sister. "What could have caused this?"

"She is beautiful," said the sister's husband to himself uneasily.

She had gone out by herself one morning in a rowboat—visiting, perhaps, or on an errand to look for driftwood or agates, or to watch the horizon where the sky and lake met, or just to be alone. As the day passed, the people began to wonder where she could be, and then to worry. Two men pulled a canoe to the water; they would look for her, they said—and then the boat appeared from around a bluff. The young woman's hair had changed to the white of the cumulous clouds that floated in the sky. Her mother helped her from the rowboat, asking her where she had been; distraught, she appeared unable to speak.

The silver-haired woman never spoke about what had happened, and never really had much to say for the rest of her life. In the way of those old-time Anishinaabe people, no one said anything to the quiet young woman about the sudden whitening of her hair; if she had wanted to talk about it, she would have. Nevertheless, they knew, and the story remained alive until only older people remembered the day her hair had changed from sable to silver; after those elders had passed on and journeyed to the next world in the west, the story had been passed to another generation and continues today. She had encountered a mishibizhii, a spirit from the lake, and was the only human to have survived the fearful experience. The sight had turned her hair to the whitest of whites.

Here in Onigamiising winters are cold. What we can see of Gichigami is covered by a thick sheet of white ice for several months of the year, though the ice does sometimes move, clearing out spaces of water that is cold to even look at. Snow covers the lake, wind blowing it to drifts of varying sizes and shapes or sometimes leaving stretches of bare ice—and then the wind direction turns, a storm blows in, and the drifts shift and re-form. It is an awesome sight whether from the shore, hillside, or top of the hill, Gichigami in winter. And that is the season, *biboon*, when we can from time to time see evidence of the mishibizhiig, the spirits who live underwater in the lake.

They live deep, deep underwater in the lake that is their home, and they rise to the surface on the coldest mornings of winter. Their breath spirals into columns that remain in place until the wind picks up, then they drift and curl, columns colliding and separating, a white mist that mimics the waves that the lake spirits create. On mornings when the sun is out, light picks up the tiniest pieces of ice within the mist; these sparkle briefly and then melt into the sheet of ice that covers the lake.

As winter moves into early spring, the ice sheet begins to melt and drift, blown away from the shore; below the surface of the lake the mishibizhiig continue their destiny, the work they were created to do, which is to watch over Gichigami. They can be protective, as the old stories tell us. Here in Onigamiising we have built a walkway along the lake, of expensive and exotic wood, strong enough to overcome the lake, we thought—and it has been pushed back by the mishibizhiig time and time again.

The June I was newly pregnant with my first baby was one of those unusual times when the ice didn't melt and move out into the lake. At noon I sat on a park bench outside the Federal Building, wearing my jacket because of the unseasonably cool air, and looked at the vastness of that white sheet of ice, a contrast to the green of trees and leaves.

That night I dreamed of the white lake and the cool air, and of my baby, a girl with soft, fine dark hair; within the softness of that hair that I stroked were four even finer gold chains. There was a significance there that I cannot explain, the holding on of that beautiful sheet of ice by the lake spirits; I felt honored to breathe that air that blew across it and onto that park bench in downtown Onigamiising.

SEA SMOKE ON GICHIGAMI

Little Spirit Moon, Great Spirit Moon,
Bear Moon, and Snow Crust Moon
           the four moons of winter

Sunrise
        these coldest mornings of gelid moons
sears the horizon, slicing dawn from night
red-orange light captured on facets of ice crystals
that spin and glitter in the air, falling
to the caul of translucent marble
that covers Gichigami.

Beneath that frozen vastness
the lake world stirs with the earth
    light diffused to the palest of golds
    rouses spirits curled in sleep
    on the valleyed lake floor; awake
    they push with scaled claws and rise
        these coldest mornings of gelid moons
their breath a song to the world above the ice.

Delicate inhalations
from the sliver of space between ice and lake
expels to white steam, sea smoke a silver mist
rising in vapor columns over the surface of the lake.

On the shore an old man lifts a hand to the morning;
      the wind lifts tobacco from his palm,
        scattering the offering in four directions
watching the song
gray white silver
drifting rolling across ice.

The song begins with spring
and the Creator who made the earth
   streams rivers lakes oceans
   grass plants flowers trees
    the medicines the seasons
   birds animals insects
and finally the first man,
born to the granddaughter of the moon.

Shimmering cold in summers of the past
the lake carried them weightless buoyant floating
   sun glinting on wet scales and claws
    on the shore they rested
    against gabbrous rock heated by the sun,
this before rancor reached the world
before the Great Flood and finally redemption
   and the retreat to the underwater,
   the cold darkness of the valley a grace of sorts.

Since then, in early autumn
when skies reflect gentian waters of the lake
   spirits rise with the tide, lured
   by the colors of the hillside
   water-blurred red orange yellow leaves
   against the black of rocky cliffs
yet obliquely they gaze, cautiously
remembering the spirit who dazzled by the brilliance
drifted lost toward an inlet
where a young woman rowing alone
in a green-painted wooden boat
recoiled, her hair whitening.

Late autumn ice forms and breaks
    heavy on the surface of the lake
    slowing the movements of the spirits
    whose scales and claws
    gray and dull starving for the sun
reach above Gichigami to grasp the wind
and on the shore waves collide
   with rocks, trees
   and fragilities built by man

In winter, cold subdues the water surface;
nights, white ice reflects the winter moons
    Little Spirit Moon, Great Spirit Moon,
    Bear Moon, Snow Crust Moon
in their slow sail through the sky.

Sunrise sears the horizon,
slicing dawn from night
    red-orange light captured on facets of ice crystals
    that spin and glitter in the air, falling
    to the caul of translucent marble ice
    that covers Gichigami
    descending to the valleyed lake floor,
rousing the spirits curled in sleep;
awakened they push with scaled claws
   ascending toward the sun
    these coldest mornings of gelid moons.
As one, then another, and others emerge
steam rises, fog glitters in the light
their breath a silver song
to the world above the ice.

BARNEY-ENJISS

MY UNCLE BARNEY was born in Chippewa City in 1921, a year or so before
the house fire that relocated his mother and the children to Duluth—
temporarily, they thought, and although the family did travel back and forth
from Duluth to Chippewa City and Grand Portage in the years that followed,
they never settled permanently in Chippewa City after that.

Barney traveled to many places in the world. He loved seeing it all, even
serving in the Merchant Marine during World War II and the Vietnam War.
My father used to say that the song "Far Away Places" made him think of
Barney every time he heard it. Grand Portage was really home to Barney
and the siblings, however, and whenever it was possible, they visited northern Minnesota in early August, to Duluth to see relatives here and then
to Grand Portage for the Rendezvous Days powwow. Barney died during
the powwow a few years ago, his spirit leaving his body to stay where it
really lived. He was buried in the small graveyard in back of the Holy Rosary
church in Grand Portage, where most of the Drouillard brothers and sisters
are buried, those who traveled the furthest returned to their father's home.

Barney was one of those likable people, affable, and good company.
When we were talking once I asked if I could write down what he was saying.

"Sure, you can," he answered. "Where was I—oh, yeah, my mother
used to say when I was making a lot of noise when I was a kid: 'Barney-
enjiss, doom biigis!' It was like, pipe down, and she was always laughing
when she said it. I didn't live with her much after I got to be a bigger kid,
maybe six, because I went away to Indian school and lived there most of the
time. That's how it was for a lot of kids then, in the 1930s. It was at school
where I got my name changed; see, Barney, that was the name I had when I
was born; my mother named me Barney but at school they said that Barney
wasn't a name from the Bible, so they called me Bernard, like that dog, you
know, the St. Bernard; I didn't like it. I went home most summers, either to
Duluth to my mother's place or sometimes to Mineral Center, up the North
Shore on Old Highway 61, not far from Chippewa City, where I was born,

and Grand Portage. Up in Mineral Center I ran wild and made noise all summer, and also helped my dad Martin Drouillard, the Old Man we called him, with his Indian Stand.

"The stand was located six miles south of Canada, on Highway 61. Drouillard's Indian Stand. Kate LeSage, my dad's friend, it was her allotment, her property. They built the stand in the early 1930s, a log building; my brothers helped build it. They made a roadside stand, too, right on the road; made of birch and decorated with birchbark. The place closed sometime during World War II, maybe, as a business, though the building stayed. When they were building the log cabin, I remember it was when I got back from government school for the summer in 1934, my dad asked mom if I could go up there for the summer, to help. Paddy was there, too, I recall; he was my mom's second husband and they got married, I think, in 1927-ish, if I am remembering it right. Bob said he and Paddy chopped cedars to build the cabin; now there's so many weeds you can't tell what was there. I have a picture of the building; I sent it to the Casino; they were asking for pictures to use on a calendar, and they paid me fifty dollars for it! I'll send you a copy. On Katie's side of the family, Pigskin Peterson took a picture of himself by the front door, of the log cabin, squatting. Pigskin, he inherited the allotment. He worked with us some; my brother Ray would say we would get a job in Cleveland or wherever, and Pigskin would show up! He'd just show up!

"The Old Man, my dad, never had much of an education, though my mother and dad met in Indian school in Vermilion. He was an entrepreneur, would sell handmade crafts that he made and other Indian people made . . . even in winter and snow, Indians would make handmade crafts and then sell them in summertime. He put in a Shell gas with a hand pump with ten gallons in front of the log building, and he put a sign on the birchbark curio stand, 'Only Indian Stand on the North Shore,' which it was when it started. More people had stands, too, a lot of them that they built in the 1930s and 1940s.

"We all worked at the stand, and other people did, too, but it was the Old Man had the idea; he was the boss. Kate sort of had the purse strings, kept track of the money—did the bookkeeping, though it was a joint venture for her and the Old Man. There was a birchbark curio stand, and besides that in the log building there was a store case, where they kept the good stuff, the good beadwork and craftwork, and a pop machine. Up the Gunflint, these Scandinavian brothers hand-carved these little woodsmen from cedar that the Old Man traded for and then resold. He was always working on something, the Old Man; sawed ice in the bay in winter, had an icehouse on the property for ice in the summer. He had an old '34 International Truck that he used to drive up the shore and up the Gunflint, selling to whoever wanted to buy, and then visiting my brother Al in Walker; Al had tuberculosis and lived a long time at Ah-Gwa-Ching Sanitarium. He was a typical Indian guy, the Old Man. He'd pack some ham and some bacon and go on the road or to work he found, and we'd stop in the woods to eat. He would work when we were on the road, taking stuff along and selling along the way, to visit Albert over at the TB hospital in Walker; it paid for gas when we went to visit Al.

"Everything they sold at the stand was original Chippewa stuff. Neighboring Indians came from Portage to Mineral Center to sell their wares and crafts. It was all original stuff, a lot of birchbark, birchbark canoes, wood fiber flowers . . . my mother made willow baskets, too, and dolls out of rags from the St. Vincent de Paul store in Duluth. The Old Man's own invention was these tomahawks or war clubs. 'I'm the Club Man,' he would call himself. He'd get the wood to make them from his place, where the Methodist church is now . . . he'd row across the bay to Hat Point to Wasnanigan Bay to get rocks for tomahawks and war clubs; they were his idea. Me and Patsy helped our mother and the Old Man paint them, then we wrapped them in newspaper and he wholesaled them all over tourist country for 15, 25, 35, 75 cents, up to two dollars. The clubs were the Old Man's original idea.

"People made what they were good at, and they sold them at the stand, and everything was original, from the woods or something that had been used before, like old clothes or tin cans, inner tubes—nothing from China! Bessie Clark, she married Joe Kadonce, they helped get willow for baskets. She made necklaces, the fronts were eight or ten layers tapered to the breast, they were her own design; she used seed beads, Indian beads. In Duluth, Paddy—your grandpa—cut the branches and Patsy and Ma made willow baskets, and I sold them, with my little brother Jerry, to people in bars in the West End, close to where we lived when we were in Duluth. Patsy and Ma took baskets to sell door-to-door out in the East End.

"Other people did this, too, of course; the Old Man built the first stand but he was not the only one doing this. Other Indians had things they made, up in Grand Portage Reservation, though they didn't sell in winter, that's when they made things; then in summer they sold. They sold to get money to get a loaf of bread.

"I don't know, personally, if tourists thought of the stuff as art. The Old Man may have when he advertised original Indian curios—that *is* art. He'd go around to resorts, for the tourist trade. As for what we made and sold, well, you'd go with the flow, with what people wanted. I helped make the clubs, but Bud and Albert were there longer and would have known more

Patsy, family friend Catherine, my grandmother Victoria,
my uncle Ray, uncle Barney, and Martin Drouillard
holding the paws of Mister Drouillard at the Indian Stand
on Old Highway 6

COURTESY OF ALBERT DROUILLARD

about making the 'good stuff' with the Old Man and our mother, and the other people who wanted to sell things at the stand. One thing, if the tourist was not buying, just looking around, and then just taking pictures of 'Old Joe,' this mannequin he made and stood by the teepee, then the Old Man would charge them 25 cents to take a picture. And they could take a picture of the dog, too, whose name was Mister Drouillard; he was a black and white part-collie, and the Old Man got him a corncob pipe with the stem wrapped to take in the mouth. You'd ask the dog, 'what's your name?' and he'd go 'RA raw RAOW roaw,' sounded like 'Mister Drouillard,' like the dog was talking.

"World War II changed everything, I guess, and the stand closed during the war, but I imagine that people still get to sell their craftwork and wares, just not at roadside stands; they do at the Grand Portage lodge today. Patsy's son Bob and his wife Karen used to do that, make things that they sold, traveled in their van; they used to have a stand at the Grand Portage powwow; they bead medallions for the different branches of the service, like for the Army, and the Marines, that are pretty nice; and they make other things, too, beadwork and leatherwork, like Bob's mother Patsy and my mother and Paddy and the Old Man, keeping up the tradition."

THE STONE TOMAHAWK

IT WAS THE SHINY PAINT JOB that drew my eye to the floor, where it lay under a wooden end table that displayed several imported resin figurines of scowling Indian chiefs and yearningly pensive maidens. The stone tomahawk, like the fanciful figures of imaginary Indians, had been bypassed by seekers of genuine Indian art and artifacts, who likely thought it a Boy Scout craft project.

And it was the shiny paint job that caused me to kneel there, on the floor of the old warehouse converted to specialty and antique shops, for a closer look. Attached to the handle, a ten- to twelve-inch length cut from a willow branch, was an irregular oval rock the size of my fist, painted with red and yellow geometrical designs, secured to the handle by a length of basswood fiber wrapped back and forth around the rock and handle in a figure eight. The entire piece had been shellacked; except for a little dust and that the wrap had become dried out and somewhat loose, it looked tourist-shop new. And familiar to me.

I have many times heard my father and my uncles talk about the tomahawks and war clubs they used to make to sell at their father's Indian tourist stand, decades ago, on Old Highway 61 that ran through the Grand Portage reservation. We have a photograph of my grandmother and aunt assembling and painting tomahawks at their kitchen table in Duluth, and packing them in a cardboard box to bring up to the reservation. Could this possibly be one of the pieces that they made for tourist trade, I wondered, and should I bring my dad downtown to see it? My father was an Ojibwe elder, born just months after the Merriam Report was released and five years before the Indian Reorganization Act; he enlisted in the newly integrated U.S. Army, married, and raised his children during the termination era from post–World War II through the 1980s (although termination was officially repeated by Congress in 1988, and in my opinion, it is still in existence). He witnessed decades of changing federal Indian policies and governmental attempts to solve the "Indian problem" that our ancestors inadvertently created by existing, and during those decades our very large extended family has survived, and often thrived. *Should I bring him to the antique mall?* Indian family histories are collective and complex, walked by ghosts of past, present, and future bearing forged chains that can rattle and clank painfully when shaken, sometimes by what might appear outside of Indian Country to be the most innocuous of questions. *Should I ask if he would like to see the stone tomahawk?*

I thought about it for a couple of days, then stopped by for coffee and asked.

He wanted to go.

Tourist season over, it was not difficult to find a parking space in Canal Park. When we got out of the car he looked briefly up toward the sky and then around him, as was his way. I expect he was looking through the buildings and cars, which are tangible yet really only temporary, placing people and happenings from earlier times. Inside the old warehouse, he lifted the stone tomahawk from the floor with two hands and looked down at it for a good minute without saying anything while I waited, touching and peering at the resin chiefs and princesses, a dried and cracking birchbark basket, the grimy gilt frame around a print of *The End of the Trail*.

I cleared my throat. "The wrap is a little loose," I said.

"That's easy to fix; a little glue would fix it, right underneath." He looked down again, past the rock, the willow handle, the paint, shellac, and basswood twine, through more than half a century. I looked, too, wishing that I could see what he saw.

"I'm going to buy this," he said.

MY FATHER'S PARENTS, who first met around 1906 at the Vermilion Lake Indian School up north near Tower, Minnesota, met again when both came to Duluth sometime before 1920. They were both Ojibwe, my grandfather from Fond du Lac Reservation and my grandmother from the Vermilion district of Bois Forte. This was, I think, the most recent migration of our family to Onigamiising, where most of us live today. We, and the tribal bands and lands of our ancestors, are part of the Ojibwe nation, which is one of the largest tribal groups in the United States and Canada. In the States, most of its 130,000 tribally enrolled members live in the upper Midwest. The Ojibwe (or Chippewa, or in our own language, Anishinaabe) are one of the many Algonquin-language–based Woodland Indian tribes, who live in areas from Maine to Minnesota and into the Dakotas. More than five hundred years ago, following dreams and visions from the Creator, the people migrated from the Newfoundland area to where we live today. Our traditions and values, our spirituality and our art, are linked to the historical Great Migration made by our ancestors, and to the land. My family—my grandmother Victoria Mellisa McKoy and her husbands Martin Drouillard and Elias LeGarde, are descendants of tribal people who made the Great Migration, whose children and grandchildren became involved in the fur trade as it moved inland. The land cession treaty of 1854 shrank the land base of northeastern Minnesota, the Arrowhead region, to the reservations each was associated with that stand today: Fond du Lac, Bois Forte (Nett Lake), and Grand Portage. Including some earlier movement from La Pointe (on Madeline Island, Wisconsin) and removals to White Earth Reservation in western Minnesota, those are the lands on which our extended families have walked, lived, left, returned, left and returned again, and loved for generations.

Respect, humility, gratitude, and the obligation to contribute to the group and the world are at the heart of traditional Ojibwe values. The old-time Ojibwe lived moderately in the place of weather extremes and left a respectfully unobtrusive footprint on the earth, moving in cycle with the four seasons to a series of camps: from winter hunting camps to spring maple sugar harvesting areas; to spring planting, summer fishing and gathering locations; to late summer wild rice harvest camps; then back to winter camps, beginning again the seasonal rhythm of work. Acknowledgment of and gratitude to the Great Spirit as the provider of life and of the Earth's resources are vital to the traditional seasonal lifestyle, which adapted to changes that came with the arrival of Europeans by the connection and inclusion of those changes into Ojibwe epistemology, and continues today. Traditional core Ojibwe values include gratitude, humility, generosity, and respect. Other related values include a great consideration for elders, resourcefulness, self-sufficiency, reflection, an extended view of time, and a sense of place in time, space, and destiny. A very simple manifesto of Ojibwe philosophy that is grounded in and has emerged from traditional values follows:

> Everything is a gift from the Creator. We are humbled by this knowledge, and grateful. We acknowledge our thanks with prayer that encompasses life, taking care of our gifts and using them resourcefully. We acknowledge that those gifts have made us rich, and that in our richness we can afford and are obligated to be generous, with both tangibles and intangibles: generosity, including a generosity of spirit, is the natural and sensible conclusion. We meet our obligation to the future by honoring the past and living a good life in the present.

This worldview, rooted in spiritual or religious beliefs, has manifested itself in the continuity and survival of the Ojibwe people—the passing on of history, religious practice, and ways of being are there in all ways of communication and expression, in storytelling, ceremony, work, leisure, and in the making of art.

So, what is Native art? I wondered. The beadwork wall-hanging of pansies made by my uncle Tommy as a special gift for his wife—that would be art, of course. How about the willow baskets made by my grandmother Vickie and sold by her children on Superior Street in the West End neighborhood of Duluth, including in the bars? My grandmother and Aunt Patsy filled them with paper artificial flowers. Were those art? Yes, I thought. The painted stone tomahawks and war clubs? Yes. And what about the toy drums made from tuna cans, covered with birchbark and red rubber cut from ruined inner tubes, can they be considered art as well? I asked my cousin Bob, who is a little older and considerably wiser than me, if there is a way to tell if an object can be actually and legitimately called American Indian art. He answered my question with a question, as is his style. "Did an Indian make it?"

I DIDN'T KNOW THE TERM "tourist art" until a local Native art collector used the term at an exhibit at the Tweed Museum of Art at the University of Minnesota Duluth, where I work. Displayed in an acrylic cube was a doll-sized teapot, cup, and saucer made of birchbark trimmed with sweetgrass. "Isn't that pretty," I thought to myself as memories of my family flowered and bloomed, unseen by everyone around me.

"That set is tourist art," he commented, "made for sale to people as a souvenir."

And I understood that there was a term that could define and include that lovely little birchbark set, and also understood in an instant that the Drouillard and LeGarde family arts—dolls made from rags, decorated birchbark baskets, beadwork, toy drums—like those arts made of other families like ours, are in a category that has no limit, really; the concept cannot be contained. For me as an Ojibwe woman who has experienced the histories and capricious government Indian policies of the twentieth century and into the twenty-first, this was a moment of pride and freedom.

How would an art expert define this type of art making? Tourist, or souvenir, art is the creation of objects intended for sale or trade to consumers outside the crafters' own tribal group or community. For the Native people of northeastern Minnesota, this type of artwork has been made since the first days of contact with the fur trade—explorers and scouts, then voyageurs, traders, and fur trading posts. Utilitarian goods needed by fur trade workers (such as moccasins, leggings, canoes, and baskets) were bought/

traded from the Ojibwe, who trapped and processed pelts in exchange for tools, kettles, woven cloth, needles, thread, silver jewelry, and beads. The Ojibwe, who had been decorating and embellishing everyday objects with their artwork since long before European contact, then integrated trade goods into their own traditional works.

The Ojibwe tourist art that was sold at the Drouillard Indian Stand was the historical descendant of the fur trading days, a combination of functional and decorative, traditional and the creative application of worldview to changes brought by European impact. The pieces varied greatly, some made in the same way and of the same materials as they had been for centuries, some from beads, paint, and nails purchased or traded for (the exchange of a pound of wild rice, or a willow basket, a pair of moccasins for cash, canned goods for household items benefited everyone involved) and some of the most interesting creations were crafted from leftovers and discards from the dump, a material demonstration of the creative resourcefulness that has made Ojibwe survival possible (and, Cousin Bob says, fun). No matter what the source of materials, in every piece was the spirit and essence of traditional Ojibwe values and ways of being. In every piece of art that was made for sale to non-Native people outside of Indian country—tourist art—are cultural, historical, sociological, and spiritual aspects far beyond what an individual can see or feel. As I tell the students in the American Indian Art class I teach, we will never know the story behind the art, where the materials came from, the life of the person who made the piece, and the journey the piece made to the place where its existence and ours intersect, whether in a museum or secondhand shop. We see or touch a tangible piece that was seen or touched by others before us; their work and spirit continue, as do we. Tourist art is the art of survival, resiliency, and creative living, grounded in traditional tribal values.

From the beginning of contact between European fur traders and the Ojibwe people here in the interior, trade/business increased constantly, accelerating in a snowball effect. Intertwined was social interaction—many Ojibwe families are extended dynasties with French surnames that date back to the fur trade era. Their lives evolved against the backdrop of treaty making and regularly changing federal Indian policies as well as historical events in and outside of their world. By the twentieth century, in a changing lifestyle and economy that had become increasingly money-based, tangibles of the seasonal lifestyle (wild rice, maple syrup, baskets, moccasins) that had in the traditional life been crafted for family or community became also a means of obtaining scarce cash money, or were traded for those goods that had become necessities (tools, plows, household goods).

When I read *Night Flying Woman*, Ignatia Broker's biographical novel of the life of her great-great-grandmother, I was struck by how similar her family's adaptations were to mine and other families I know: forced relocation to a smaller land base after treaty negotiations and the introduction of a cash-based economy resulted in a scarcity of food and living necessities that had traditionally been carefully planned and harvested. The response of Broker's family was to make cedar and rush mats, baskets, moccasins, and beaded artwork that would be sold for cash or traded for household goods. Many families did the same: those time-honored Ojibwe values that include self-sufficiency, resourcefulness, and cultural adaptation to protect and maintain tradition have served us well since the days of the ancestors; applied to changes in land and lifestyle, they meant that we could and would survive. I have thought many times about the decisions made by our grandparents and great-grandparents—Ignatia Broker's, mine, and other Ojibwe people's—and the combination of tenacity and resilience that brought us to where we are today. Where to compromise, where to stay unmoving?

The Drouillard Indian Stand was on the Grand Portage Reservation, six miles south of the Canadian border, a half mile inland from the shores of Lake Superior on Old Highway 61, which has for the past half century or so been a back road. Drouillard ancestors lived there before the fur traders arrived; Drouillard descendants live there or nearby today.

Martin Drouillard was born in 1885, less than thirty years after the upheavals and resettlements of the 1854 land cession treaty. He and his wife Victoria attended Indian boarding schools, both church and government. As their six children reached school age, they attended a number of different Indian boarding schools in Minnesota and Wisconsin. Victoria's second husband, my grandfather Elias LeGarde, also attended several different Indian boarding schools; one of these was the Vermilion Lake Indian School, where Martin and Victoria had also been students. Elias had known Martin and Victoria since their days at Vermilion. My father Jerry and his brother, my uncle Tommy, were Victoria and Elias's children, her youngest. Elias was a maker of traditional and tourist arts also, and sometimes worked at the Drouillard stand.

An artist and entrepreneur, Martin traveled throughout northern Minnesota and Wisconsin and other parts of the upper Midwest in a pickup truck packed with wild rice, maple sugar, baskets, and craftwork made by himself, his relatives, and friends. He sold to "anyone who wanted to buy," as my uncle Bob put it, individuals as well as resorts and stores that would then mark up for resale. After Martin and several of his sons built the log cabin and birchbark-covered roadside stand on Old Highway 61, he continued through the mid-1950s to travel in his pickup truck with goods to sell to stores, resorts, and individuals; he enjoyed travel, visiting, meeting people, and negotiating trades and sales.

Like that of several other families in the area, the Drouillard family life of barter, travel, and building and maintaining relationships to people outside the family and community was in many ways a continuation of the traditional seasonal lifestyle, and subsistence and survival through adaptation and resiliency that began long before European contact and sustained the Ojibwe people through the fur trade era, the land losses and relocations during the treaty era, the upheavals of the Indian boarding school days that were followed by the federal termination policies—and continues today.

Martin's plan was to attract tourists and travelers who wanted to acquire American Indian–made objects that were curious, rustic, authentic, or all three. For many people who stopped at the stand, the purchase of art as a souvenir (much of it made specifically for sale to them) symbolized more than a memento from a trip: for some it was a way to "try on" or pretend that they were American Indians themselves, for some a search for fulfillment of a deep need as an immigrant society to be part of the essence of the land and country—to be part of a history and experience, secondhand though it might be, through the purchase of a physical object from people indigenous to the land. For the people who Uncle Albert, Martin's son, described as "the more serious buyer," and his grandson Bob as "collectors, the people who knew what they were looking for," Martin kept "the good stuff, the really good beadwork, baskets, or leatherwork" in a store case inside the log cabin.

As a continuation of cultural values, adaptation, and resilience that began with European impact, the entrepreneurship of Indian stands was more than a crass sale of goods, the desperation of people in need; it certainly was not an abandonment of traditional tribal ways and values. The making and sale of arts and crafts, tourist and traditional, contributed to the survival of the Ojibwe far beyond the putting of food on the table. Traditional work culture, applied to the creation and sale of tourist art, played a role in the cohesiveness of families and communities. In the Ojibwe worldview there is a strong awareness of the obligation of the individual to make a contribution to the group; for many, the cooperation necessary for success in the tourist art business reinforced the strength of the family and community groups while providing a driving force in the preservation of traditional arts as well as experiments with new.

Martin in front of the Indian Stand
COURTESY OF ALBERT DROUILLARD

My dad's older brothers and sister moved away from Minnesota during the 1950s and 1960s, during the peak years of the federal government's termination policies, designed to end the political status and sovereignty of tribes. With encouragement and sometimes financial incentives from the Federal Relocation Program, many American Indian people relocated to urban areas—among these were Seattle, Tacoma, and Los Angeles, which is where several Drouillard family members settled. They know northeastern Minnesota as homeland and home, however; my dad's siblings visited as often as they could, and their children's generation, my cousins who are, like me, now the grandparent generation, care for that love of home in their children and grandchildren. Grand Portage, Chippewa City, and Duluth, those places of woods and rock, each of them on the North Shore of vast and cold Lake Superior, are what we are made from: surely, this must be in the very DNA of generations of an extended family and community eating the fish and game, the foods and medicines from the woods, inhaling and exhaling the same air as do the animals and plants. This surely has resulted in an existence that is a connection more than symbiotic.

Material for the making of arts and crafts came from many sources, some the same as those used by earlier generations and some from the times, from the woods and lakeshore, from worn household goods and clothing past their original use, from the Used-a-Bit store in downtown Duluth and the dump; as a last resort from the dime store or hardware store—through scavenge, purchase, or barter—the materials passed through the hands of the Drouillard extended family and became art, molded by the hands, hearts, and histories of all who touched them. Purchasers became part of that history, and the story, of each piece. The origin of a miniature canoe, made as a Christmas tree ornament, was the birch tree and hands carefully peeling bark for a basket, in the fashion learned by watching others peel bark; it was hands tracing and cutting a pattern and sewing the tiny *jimaan*, looping the end of the thread or sinew to create a hanger; it was hands setting the ornament out on the birchbark roadside stand; it was hands, perhaps from a motorist or a child riding in the car to see the sights of the woods along the North Shore, picking it up and deciding to purchase, perhaps with a pack of Black Jack gum. What came of these materials from the woods and lakes, from the hardware store and the Used-a-Bit store, from the dump, or from trade and barter with store owners, farmers, and friends?

In the same way that not everyone knows all of the traditional Ojibwe stories, not all of the family and friends who made art to sell at the Indian Stand knew how to make every object, and in that traditional worldview each person had a gift or talent that they could contribute. One person might be skilled at harvesting birchbark, black ash, or willow, another a skilled basket maker. Smaller pieces of birchbark were made into souvenir miniature canoes or baskets, Christmas tree ornaments, small figurines, etched squares or rectangles meant to hang on a wall, and postcards with those same etched designs. Several people were beaders who made freehand chains, bracelets and necklaces, or loomed belts, bracelets, and bags, or could appliqué floral Ojibwe designs onto bags and medallions. Some could hunt and trap, and tan hides and pelts; some made moccasins, bags, and jewelry from deer or moose hide. My grandmother made dolls from scraps from the Used-a-Bit store, trimmed with leather, beads, yarn, and horsehair. Martin and the boys made souvenir drums of tin cans covered with birchbark; the drum heads were red rubber from blown inner tubes, laced with strips of hide or the same red inner tube. Martin's clubs were made by several people; my grandmother and aunt painted some of them at their kitchen table. And wild rice was sold, of course; and maple syrup, and maple sugar candies. No matter what the materials and where they came from, as Uncle Barney said, "Everything at the Indian Stand was authentic; it was the genuine thing, made by real Indians."

WHEN YOU ARE WALKING, along the lakeshore or in the woods, when you see a stone in a nice oval, or square or oblong, one that you can picture in a tomahawk that you will make, bring it home and save it. When you pick it up, acknowledge and give thanks to the Creator and to the spirit of the stone, which is moving because of you.

During *niibin*, summer, after the sap has finished running but before the cooler, shorter days of early *dagwaagin*, autumn, will cause the tree to change color, cut from a healthy popple or from willow branches that are the thickness of a man's thumb. As you have been taught, pray your acknowledgment and thanks to the Creator and the tree, and put down tobacco. Cut the branches to lengths of about a foot. Drill a hole through the branch at one end, an inch below where you will attach the stone.

Buy or trade for a can of shellac, a paintbrush, and paint (red, green, yellow, black). If you do not have *zhooniyaa*, money, bring a sack of wild rice, or a jar of maple syrup, or a doll made out of scraps of secondhand clothing, to trade at the store. Paint the stone in patterns and designs.

When you cut down a basswood tree for firewood or for building, acknowledge that the tree is giving its life to you, and give thanks. Leave tobacco. When you cut it further for its uses, set aside the bark. While it is still pliable and soft, gently pull the fibers of the inner bark into thick threads that you store in a place they will not dry out. Use the basswood fiber soon; it must be flexible for ease while working it.

Attach the stone to the top of the branch handle with a length of basswood fiber that you wrap around the stone and through the hole in the handle, around and back and forth, snug but not too tight. Knot and wrap it under the stone. Because the fiber will shrink and tighten as it dries, let it alone, at least overnight.

Shellac the entire tomahawk, and let it dry.

Display it on the counter of the Indian Stand, where it will catch the eye of a tourist, or trade it for something you want. To a store owner for flour, coffee, a length of calico. Or to your cousin, for a pair of pliers or a bag of seed beads, that you will give to your sister to appliqué onto a deerskin bag that she will sell at the Indian stand. Your cousin will trade the tomahawk to a farmer, for a cast-iron kettle, that he will give to his mother. Or you might trade the tomahawk to the owner of a gas station and general store in Grand Rapids, for gas that will get the pickup truck to Ah-Gwa-ching, the tuberculosis sanitarium, where you are driving to visit your son. The owner of the gas station will sell the tomahawk to a schoolteacher, who will hang it on the wall of her classroom. Your thin and frail son will lose one ulcerated lung and then, surprisingly, outlive you all.

Later, from the spirit world, walk with your feet that are lighter than dust over the scarred wooden floors of a bowery warehouse converted to an antique depot, where an elder Ojibwe man holds the stone tomahawk in two hands and gazes through decades at his sister painting tomahawks at a kitchen table, and at his mother packing them in a cardboard box to bring to the Indian Stand. His daughter's mortal fingers brush over a resin Indian maiden, over a dry and cracked birchbark basket, over the grimy gilt frame around an *End of the Trail* print; as she turns back toward her father, her earthbound feet step clumsily into your spirit space, causing chains of vapor to sway and rattle soundlessly. *Do you hear that?* she doesn't ask. Over the stir she clears her throat.

"The wrap is a little loose," she says.

"That's easy to fix; a little glue would fix it, right underneath," he answers in his soft and husky voice. The grace of his years calms the chains, which still and silence.

"I'm going to buy this," he says.

PART III
RABBITS IN WINTERTIME

LISTENING AND REMEMBERING BY HEART

IN OJIBWE ORAL TRADITION, stories about the creation of the world and how the earth came to be the way it is today are told during the winter months, when there is snow on the ground. The time-honored reason for this is consideration for animals and birds who are hibernating or away in that cold season; they will not hear us talking about them and thus won't be embarrassed or uncomfortable. Of course, there are other stories (romances, mysteries, funny stories, ghost stories) that can be told any time of the year, but we always take great care in observing the wintertime oral tradition. In doing so, we continue what our grandparents' generation learned from their own grandparents: our spiritual beliefs, history, and the life journey of Bimaadiziwin, the living of the good life.

The stories are a gift with reason and purpose. There are lessons in the wintertime stories, and explanations. They are the foundation of Ojibwe religious beliefs and entertaining, and they are interwoven with the stories of our ancestors' lives as well as our own. Nanaboozhoo made foolish, selfish mistakes; he acted heroically and with compassion; so did our grandparents, and so do we. Like the ancestors, we are reliving the sacred stories every day, and as it was with them, the stories have become part of us and we have become part of the stories.

When my aunt Carol talked with me about the travel of our ancestors from Madeline Island to Fond du Lac and the American Fur Post, we both understood that our own family saga was a continuation of the Great Ojibwe Migration from the east, the journey undertaken because of dreams and visions sent by the Creator. She wondered about the earlier part of the journey, what it was like on the long trip from the East Coast along the Great Lakes to Madeline Island and the unseen but true interweaving of religious teachings with the necessities of survival during the concurrent snowball effects of fur trade workers pouring into North America. She mentioned marriages between fur trade employees and the women in our family, some by the Catholic missionaries and some under no legal or church auspices at all. Some of our great-great-grandmothers were abandoned by their husbands, who then legally married Euro-American women. It was always hard for women, always, and our grandmothers had terrible experiences at boarding school when they were just young girls.

This bothered Aunt Carol greatly as she spoke, then she sat up straight and said that we couldn't know why these things happened but they were meant to be. She wanted me to know these things, she said, and she wanted me to remember. There were so many stories and yet so much missing, so much to remember and so much absence to mourn. Eventually, this is what I learned: that Aunt Carol saw all of the stories past and present, spiritual and romantic, ghostly and mysterious as interwoven; that our lives, hers and mine, were a small part of a much larger story. She told me what she remembered and thought about, and I listened and learned to remember by heart.

RABBITS IN THE SNOW

WHEN I SEE THIS it is by moonlight, rabbits sitting on top of the snow outside in the middle of the night when I can't sleep, or when something wakes me up—the house framework cracking and snapping in the cold, or the furnace kicking in, interrupting a dream. I get up out of bed and walk to the window to look outside, and the times I see them, the night is still and so are they, their legs folded beneath their bodies and their ears down.

They are there to watch over us, I have heard. When I see them on winter nights, I think of Nanaboozhoo, who was at birth a white bunny rabbit. In his name we can hear the connection to the word for rabbit, *waaboos*. A small rabbit is a bunny, a *waaboosoons*, and this has been my oldest daughter's nickname since she was a little girl. Waaboosoons has another name that was given to her when she was a teenager, but I am especially fond of her childhood name because it reminds me of those days. How long a time span there has been between the birth of that tiny *waaboos* and his naming, and my daughter's birth and her naming, we don't know; what we do know is that the stories about Nanaboozhoo usually begin with *mewinzha* (a long time ago).

So, this is the way I heard it as it was continued from an earlierstory—and within the story perhaps the mystery of how much of this still happens today.

NIIZH ODAIN

THE WOLF *and* THE RABBIT

Life began for ma'ingan and his older twin Nanaboozhoo in a sudden storm with skies and clouds that darkened to purple and near black and an icy wind that blew down from the north on a mild day during early harvest season.

This is how it happened, and it still happens this way sometimes.

The Moon and Her Daughter

Mewinzha, a long time ago, Dibiki Giizis the moon and her many children lived in harmony high in the sky. Their life was busy and full, and the moon taught them all that she knew about how to live—they could keep house and hunt; they could tan hides and make clothing; they could garden and forage; they could preserve food and cook. The girls especially were close to their mother and to each other; they learned from the moon to live good lives, to honor and treat each other well, to be thrifty and respectful of their surroundings. At the same time, the moon encouraged her daughters to make time for play, and to be physically active in their games.

"Weweni," she would say as the girls set snares and chopped wood. "Carefully, do it carefully."

"Weweni," she would say as the girls rushed about the sky, playing their favorite games of tag and footracing. "Be careful, take care." She was worried about many things, as mothers are, but especially about a hole in the sky that was some distance from their house. The girls were not allowed to play anywhere near it. "After all," the moon said to the girls, "you have an entire sky to play in, so stay away from that place—it is too dangerous." This made the area attractive to the girls, of course, and so they occasionally raced around the hole when their mother wasn't watching.

For the longest time it seemed that their life of harmonious and productive work and play might continue forever, but at some point, a small discontent took root among several of the sisters over a favoritism shown by the moon to one of the girls over something none of them could later remember. This became an envy that began to grow, and to spread, and because they looked for more signs of this favoritism, they found them. "Did you see that our mother gave to her the most tender piece of meat from the pot?" one sister murmured to another. Another whispered that she noticed that the favored sister was allowed to finish cleaning the yard before it was completely clear; another that the girl was praised by the moon for her skill in making moccasins—and that her own moccasin making was never even looked at by the moon. This discontent fed upon itself until the girls felt heartsick at the neglect and poor treatment that they felt they experienced. Finally, they agreed that things would have to change—where and when they didn't yet know, but change would come when the proper time came.

Sometime after that, on a late afternoon when chores were finished, the favored sister asked if anyone would like to race.

The sisters would. "Let's make this the biggest race of all this time!" said one excitedly.

Said another, "Let us race around the hole in the sky!"

"We will go around four times," decided one of the older sisters, "and whoever finishes first will be the big winner, and she will be that forever—the fastest sister."

"And the bravest!"

The girls were excited at this, and gathered at one end of the hole. They jumped up and down, warming up for the run, and lined up, giggling and panting.

"Go!" shouted the oldest sister, and the sisters ran around the hole three times, the pack stringing out and then tightening, each girl sometimes ahead, sometimes behind, as though the running was for its own enjoyment and not for competition, but on the fourth circle one girl took the lead—the sister who had been seen as the favorite. As she neared the end of the fourth circle, the others began to tap her on the shoulder or back—in encouragement or congratulations, perhaps, but perhaps not. And who knows which sister was the one to tap just a little more forcefully, or at the right time, to cause the girl to misstep and fall over the edge of the hole and down into the darkness of the late-afternoon sky?

And just like that, she was gone, and the sisters ringed the hole in the sky, their bright faces shining down into what looked like nothingness as they searched for her; then looking at one another, they asked, "What have we done?"

The Fall from the Sky

As she fell for a long time, past clouds that drifted across the sky that grew darker as night approached and then lighter as day broke, the young woman kept her head and was not afraid. Falling through air that was at times calm, at times windy, she spread her arms like wings and felt as though she was flying. Eventually, she could see land below getting closer and closer, which proved that she was indeed falling; still she kept her calm, and when she landed, she was unhurt. Remembering what she had learned from her mother, she looked around for what she would need for shelter and water; there was a lakeshore nearby, she saw. She gathered some sheets of birchbark, some pine branches, and sheets of moss from a maple tree and carried them to the shore; from these she put together a small bed of soft moss on the top of the pine branches, and covered her small shelter with a dome of birchbark. It was there she slept for that first night, and in the morning she began her new life on the earth.

With all that the earth provided, the young woman was able to survive, and remembering her mother's teachings, she thrived in her environment, sheltered and fed. Sometime not long after she had begun her new life, she felt a flutter of movement from within her body; cupping her hands over her abdomen that had become rounder and fuller, she realized that she was expecting a baby. Thankful at the prospect of the new person, she took care to eat well and to stay active and strong, and when the baby was born, a girl, she rejoiced. Her love for the tiny one, the first daughter of the earth who she called Kwesens, was great, and she vowed to take the best care she could, and to protect her daughter from any possible harm.

Thus, Kwesens was sheltered from the time she was born; her mother was cautious and kept her close to the house while she went out alone to trap, fish, forage, and garden. The girl, always small, did not become as strong physically as her mother, but she had artistic talents: she kept a neat and pleasant house that she decorated inside with the birchbark baskets she made, and outside with wildflowers that she transplanted from outside the fence to next to the doorway. And she was born with a gift of music: before she even began to talk, she sang in a voice that was more beautiful than birdsong, her mother thought. "I am truly a fortunate woman," she said to herself one evening when, after a hard day of setting snares, she neared the house listening to her daughter sing her cooking song. "How thankful I am to have been given this gift of Kwesens," she thought when the girl sang her soft, silvery wake-up song with the robins.

And the two lived contentedly over the years as the mother's hair began to gray and the daughter grew from infancy to childhood and then young womanhood, more loved every day. As Kwesens approached young womanhood, her mother thought that the time was approaching when she would look around to see if other people lived on the earth, and to perhaps find the girl a husband who would treasure and honor her sweetness. "Soon I will talk with her about these things," the mother thought to herself. "Not yet, but soon . . ."—she felt a sadness at the thought of the girl leaving—"and I will be happy for her."

As a little child, Kwesens had been content to stay in the house and around the yard, but as she grew older and blossomed like the wildflowers, she became curious about the world outside and began to ask about it. Her curiosity was only fed by the answers her mother gave as she described the colors and sizes of different kinds of trees and plants in the forest, and the variety of birds and animals, and she began to ask to go to see these for herself. The prospect of Kwesens meeting a husband and leaving was a heaviness on her mother's mind. She answered vaguely, "Not yet, but soon . . ."

Kwesens tried to be patient, but then her questions became insistent and begging, and although the words were spoken in her voice that was music lovelier than birds singing, the mother found herself close to snapping at her daughter. Finally, she relented.

"All right," she said. "Tomorrow. In the morning you can come with me to dig up some potatoes in the field where I planted some a while ago; they should be ready."

"Oh, thank you, Mother!" the girl was joyful. "I am going to be such a help to you from now on—you won't have to work so hard, and I will take care of so many things! We will have so much fun; I can hardly wait for the morning!" and she sang her going-to-sleep song twice before sinking into her dreams.

The Conception and Birth of the Brothers

They left the house early the next morning, while the birds were still singing, and Kwesens hummed along with their song, interrupting herself every once in a while to point out, as though she had never seen such things before, how tall the pine trees were, how clear and blue the sky, how warm and sweet-smelling the breeze. At the edge of a field, the mother stopped and nodded in the direction of two branches a small distance apart that she had set into the ground to mark the planting. "There is where we will dig," she said, "you at this branch and I at the other. We will carry the potatoes home in our shawls."

The girl took off her shawl and held it away from her body, dancing. "I will help you every day from now on, Mother," she said, dipping from side to side.

"Don't go wandering away," said the mother. "You don't know your way around here and could get lost." And she walked to the other side of the field, where she laid her shawl on the ground and, kneeling, began to dig.

After first whirling around with her shawl held out from her arms like wings, Kwesens worked industriously. She lightly tossed her shawl to the ground and then knelt as her mother did, digging with a small wooden trowel to search for potatoes. She carefully brushed the dirt from each one and laid it gently on the shawl. "This one looks like it has a face. How funny," she said to herself, and was going to call over to her mother to tell her, but in the short time it took Kwesens to take in a breath, the sun was blocked by dark purple clouds the color of bruises, and the blue sky deepened to purple, then to a midnight without stars. At her back she felt and heard an icy force; before she could turn her head, the North Wind, who had been watching and waiting for how long—days, perhaps years—swept the girl up off the ground and enveloped her in a whirlwind; bound, the girl spun, and as the wind roared *you are mine* at her ears, she called, "Mother! Help me!"

> Trees whistle a warning and look to the sky
> as shivering stones dance in liquid blue field
> and listening moccasins warily step
> soft up, soft up and a turn, then freeze
> as the North Wind seizes the night.
>
> An ice snake winds past Old Woman Moon
> his cloudless stealth feinting gusts of breath
> and shocked stars rue their jealous past
> watching First Daughter spin on the edge of the world
> as the North Wind takes the night.

Hearing the fright and horror in her daughter's voice, the mother ran toward the whirlwind from which only Kwesens's hands could be seen, her body spinning madly and her outstretched arms as helpless as the wings of a captive bird.

Against the growling scream of the North Wind the girl's mother reached with her arms into the spinning column of icy air and grabbed the girl's hands. She pulled, pulled, lost her grip on one of the hands, and felt her own feet lifting from the ground, found her daughter's waist and again pulled, pulled, and the girl and her mother fell to the ground, where they pressed their bodies against the earth, which held and sheltered them from the North Wind's angry gust. He roared one last time and flew back into the sky, leaving frost on the grass that melted as the clouds parted and disappeared, and the sun shone once again.

Kwesens was helped to her feet by her mother, who could say only, "Shall we go home?"

"Yes, Mother, let us go home," the young woman answered, but she was unsteady and had difficulty walking; the way home took much longer than the way to the field had, and when she entered the house, Kwesens lay on her bed, where she slept until the next morning. When she woke, she listened to the birds without singing herself; and she did not ask to leave the house again. When invited by her mother to come along to gather medicines, or berries, she declined; quiet and fearful, she slept during the daytime and stayed awake during the night.

In a short time, the mother noticed that changes were happening to her daughter, that the girl's stomach was growing. She was obviously pregnant, and her pregnancy was progressing very rapidly. This caused the mother much concern: she prepared as well as she could for the unusual event and worried even more when she began to hear faint voices from her daughter's body. They seemed to be arguing.

"Niin nitum," said one. "My turn."

"Gaawiin; niin nitum," said the other. "No, my turn."

"Gaawiin, giin nitum," from the first. "No, your turn."

"Giin nitum. Noongoom," from the second. "Your turn. Right now."

As the argument continued, Kwesens, sleepless, grew larger and more uncomfortable and her mother's worries increased. At last, one morning Kwesens went into a labor that was long and arduous, not eased by the strengthening teas that her mother prepared. The mother prayed silently as she gently rubbed her daughter's back and sprinkled bits of maple sugar onto her tongue; mother and daughter held hands and prayed. Exhausted, neither noticed if it was daylight or dark when the first baby was born, and the mother became Nokomis, grandmother, a great and immediate joy, but she was astonished that the baby was a tiny white rabbit. Holding him in two hands, she could have gazed at this wonder forever, but she saw that her daughter was in distress and need; she set him down on a rush mat and covered him with a birchbark basket made by Kwesens, to keep him contained and safe.

Nokomis turned all of her attention to her daughter, and in the midst of tremendous difficulty the second baby born was a little wolf, Ma'ingan; however, his grandmother had no time to greet him. In the moment that she held him in her hands she saw that Kwesens, who was in a very bad way, appeared to be dying. Distracted, she stepped to the doorway of the little hut and tossed the baby wolf outside and then turned her attention to Kwesens, praying desperately as she applied all that she had learned from her own mother in trying to save her daughter's life.

"Mother, Dibiki Giizis, watch over us," she said aloud, and repeated the words as she watched the color leave her girl's face and the light leave her eyes.

Kwesens had died and Nokomis had no more to say.

Nokomis

Mewinzha, after the moon's daughter had been unable to prevent her own daughter from dying during the birth of her own twins, she had little time to mourn at first because of the tasks she had to do by herself. During the four days before burial, she prayed, encouraging the girl's spirit in her four-day walk to the west; praying, she gathered birchbark and looked for the place in the woods—she chose a place on the south side of an outcropping of black gabbrous rock, sheltered from the North Wind, near wildflowers—cowslips, wild roses, and forget-me-nots that would bloom every year during the spring and summer. "Sun and daylight will touch this place every day, my mother the moon will see this place every night that she is out," she said to her solitary self. "The leaves of the birches and poplars nearby will flutter in the breeze, sparkling by sunlight and moonlight like my sisters the stars. And the birch trees—I begin my prayer of thanks for their spirits for this— they will provide the bark that will wrap my girl's body in sweetness that will surround her as she becomes again part of the earth."

On the fourth day, the girl was buried; inside the folded sheets of birchbark her mother had tenderly bent her head to rest on her arms, which were folded atop her drawn-up knees, thus returning her to the fetal position of her existence before birth. The last she did for her daughter was to place a stick into the ground to mark the grave, knowing that over time the stick would deteriorate and fall onto the earth, that the surrounding trees would grow and perhaps shade the wildflowers' home, that perhaps the wild roses would be replaced by swamp lilies—that is the way it was in long ago days, and it still is today for many Anishinaabe people, who mark graves in this impermanent fashion.

Then the daughter of the moon returned to the birchbark hut she had shared with her only child; it seemed cavernous and empty, the rounded walls and the woven rush mats on the floor absorbing her sighs. In silence she looked at her girl's bed, smoothed and empty; at the two bowls carved out of a maple burl, only one to be eaten from; in silence she listened for a bird to warble from outside that might bring the sound of her daughter's singing to the memory that was fading so rapidly. "Nothing," she thought to herself. "There is nothing here; the world is empty," resigning herself to the void that would be the remainder of her own life. But then, through the crushing silence of her grief, a sound intruded—a faint scratching that might have been the wind blowing a twig against the outside of the wigwam. She walked to the doorway and circled the hut, but saw nothing. Back inside, she sat again and resumed her thoughts, and again the scratching interrupted their silence. "Can I not grieve my daughter without this noise?" she asked aloud. "Is my loss not enough, must my grief, all I have left of her, be interrupted in this way?" She began to search through the house, behind the beds, shaking out the hides used for blankets and to cover the doorway, lifting the rush mats, straightening the baskets . . . and then noticed the *makak*, the birchbark basket that was not stacked with the others but set upside down on a mat that was on the other side of her daughter's bed. "Oh," she breathed, and lifted the basket. There on the rush mat was the baby rabbit, where she had left him in the moments after he was born, and where in the stress of an arduous childbirth and death her mind had placed him out of her awareness.

She picked up the rabbit and held him in her cupped hands. His eyes, frightened and hopeful, took in everything, as is the way of rabbits; his nose twitched and his ears stood up—would he jump from her hands and flee? Bringing him closer to her face, she breathed on his soft white fur, which seemed to soothe him.

"Ahhhhh, Nanaboozhoo," she said. "Nanaboozhoo, I am Nokomis; I am your grandmother."

So, Nanaboozhoo was brought up by his grandmother, who although she had not expected a white rabbit as a grandchild, loved him and accepted his unusual form without question—after all, it is not up to us to question Creator-given gifts. She was soon even more surprised, however, when it became obvious that Nanaboozhoo had an even more unusual quality: he could change his shape and appearance at will. She might put him to bed as a toddler; working on a new pair of moccasins for his growing feet she would listen to his little-boy snores and smooth his hair (how she loved the smell of sun and lake wind on his hair) down before going to bed herself; in the morning he might be nowhere in the birchbark hut and Nokomis would search outside, hoping he had not gone into the woods alone and become lost. "Nanaboozhoo," she called, nearly tearful at the thoughts going through her head. "Little grandson, where are you?" From high in a tree a robin warbled his morning song that was so much like her daughter's voice that Nanaboozhoo had inherited. The song shifted to a light laugh and a call back, "I'm up here, Grandmother!" from the robin who was Nanaboozhoo, who had risen before the dawn to watch the world wake from the highest place in the yard.

Nokomis taught Nanboozhoo everything she knew in the best way she could, by telling him stories, letting him watch her work, and allowing him time to think about the meanings of stories and how things are done; when the time seemed right, he tried things out for himself. Although he made mistakes and had quite a number of lapses in judgment, by the time Nokomis was very old and her strength lessening, Nanaboozhoo could cook, keep house, hunt, fish, and trap; he could tan hides and make his own clothes; he knew the names of the medicines, of the trees and plants, and he knew languages and habits of the animals, birds, and fish; and at the very foundation of things—although this was interwoven with his failures and foolishness as a human being—he respected and honored Nokomis, knowing that women are the source of life and that *mindimoyeg*, older women, have the wisdom and power of their experience.

It gave Nokomis pleasure to see that Nanaboozhoo was learning, and would continue to learn. How Nokomis loved to listen to him sing in the morning after he had made sure that she was warm and comfortable and had enough food and water before going about the work that was his destiny, which was to walk the world. His song faded as he walked further into the woods or up the lakeshore; it returned faintly, then louder, as he made his way back home.

Guided by Nokomis, as Nanaboozhoo grew to become the powerful spirit being, half human and half North Wind, he acquired great strengths and wisdom that throughout his existence were interwoven with human weaknesses and foolhardiness—all tempered by the gentle love of his mother that was present in him from the time he was in the womb, and the practical and fierce love from Nokomis, there from the first time she held her tiny white rabbit grandson in her cupped hands.

But what of Ma'ingan, the second baby who was Nanaboozhoo's younger twin brother?

Little Brother

As a child, Nanaboozhoo learned from his grandmother how to cook, keep the house and yard tidy, and mend clothing. Each skill he learned was by watching Nokomis and listening to her stories and instructions; when he had given thought to these things, he then tried them for himself and, with practice, improved. One day, he hoped, he would be a hunter and warrior who would defend Nokomis and keep her well supplied with meat. He began to ask when the time would come that he would learn to hunt.

Nokomis made for Nanaboozhoo a child-sized bow and a handful of arrows and told him that he could play with them as practice for when he was older. She told him that the bow and arrows were not toys, however, and were not to be used to kill small animals and birds. "Do you see that small bush over there, with the thick branches set so close to the ground? Shoot your arrows into it; you will be able to practice your aim and speed, and also be able to retrieve the arrows and not lose them."

Happy with the bow and arrows and promising Nokomis that he would take good care of them, Nanaboozhoo practiced close to the house where he would be in his grandmother's sight, aiming, shooting, and then walking to the bush to retrieve the arrows. He imagined, in the way of little boys, that he was aiming at a deer, then a moose. "Ha!" he shouted in triumph when he downed the biggest animal yet, an elk, with one shot, and danced a small warrior dance on his way to retrieve the arrow. "Ha!" he shouted again as he reached into the bush and grasped the end of the arrow.

The great hunter Nanaboozhoo imagined himself to be pulling masterfully at the arrow. And he lost his grip as the arrow pulled back. He pulled again, somewhat tentatively, and again the arrow pulled back. "Are you playing with me?" he asked the bush, which didn't reply; the arrow remained in its tangled branches. "Well, don't answer, then," he huffed. Grasping the end of the arrow in two hands, he yanked as hard as he could. The arrow loosened, and out trotted a young wolf who had been holding the other end.

It was Ma'ingan, and when he opened his mouth his words were understood by the boy in the way it was in those times, when animals and humans could speak to each other. "I was teasing you, Nanaboozhoo," he said.

Although from that moment Nanaboozhoo felt that he had always known Ma'ingan, he wondered that the young wolf would know his name. He invited Ma'ingan to come meet Nokomis, his wonderment increasing as they walked the paths toward home—Ma'ingan seemed to know the way, never hesitating at the forks but walking steadily at Nanaboozhoo's side.

Nokomis was waiting in the doorway, watching as the boy and the wolf approached the birchbark hut. "Ah, welcome, Ma'ingan," she said. Graciously, in the way of Ojibwe *mindimoyeg* she invited him to come and sit, and asked if he was hungry. "Biindigen; namadabin . . . Gi bakade ina?" and when they had settled, she told Nanaboozhoo and Ma'ingan the story of their birth, and apologized to her grandson wolf. "Will you come live with us now?" she asked.

But Ma'ingan declined. Thanking Nokomis for her offer he said that he would remain living on his own, but that he would want to see them often. His decision was respected, and he was told by Nokomis that he would always be welcome, that the birchbark hut would always be his home. There was no need for further discussion: it was understood by all that the trauma he had experienced—being thrown away, the loss of mother, grandmother, and brother, and living on his own, by himself, could not be undone. It had become a part of Ma'ingan, and of Nokomis and Nanaboozhoo, also. And of the earth and the way things unfolded in the story of what would be his too-short life; it has become a part of us all that although Nanaboozhoo and Ma'ingan became the closest of brothers and dearest of friends, the wolf is a loner and does not live among humans. Since that time so long ago, Ma'ingan and his bloodline have lived with the self-reliance and contemplation that comes with solitude. This is not a bad thing or a good thing; it is simply the way of the world. It is perhaps one of the reasons for Nanaboozhoo's conflict with the mishibizhiig that his actions lacked the judgment that comes with contemplation.

Ma'ingan and the Mishibizhiig

On very cold mornings columns of steam occasionally rise from the ice that covers the big lake in wintertime; these drift together to form a fog that eventually disappears from wind or sun. Below the surface is the source of the phenomenon: the mishibizhiig, lake spirits. Much of the changing of the lake's surface, which ranges from glassy calm to roaring waves, is created by the mood and activity of the mishibizhiig, who are powerful and easily provoked. In teaching her grandson the ways of the world, Nokomis cautioned him about the mishibizhiig, telling him that they are touchy and don't like to be bothered. As a small boy, Nanaboozhoo teased the mishibizhiig when Nokomis wasn't looking by throwing rocks into the water, laughing when the annoyed spirits returned the joke with angry waves; on hot summer days when the spirits pulled themselves from the lake onto the rocks to dry and warm their cold, heavy bodies, he climbed a nearby tree and, hidden by leaves, shot small rocks onto their heads and bodies, causing them a lack of rest that further aggravated their annoyance at the boy. And as time passed and Nanaboozhoo grew to young adulthood, his teasing increased, as did the rancor between him and the mishibizhiig, until the teasing and retaliation grew to anger and hatred. Eventually, each wished to destroy the other.

It was not unusual for Ma'ingan to stop by the birchbark hut on his way to or from his house in the woods, and so on the evening of the night that he would die, Nokomis welcomed him as usual, inviting him to come inside and sit; when Nanaboozhoo arrived, they shared what was in the pot, likely stewed meat, and visited for a while as they enjoyed the warmth of the fire and the food digesting inside their filled stomachs. What did they talk about? Nokomis wondered later. Was there anything in the conversation, in the motions they made of dishing up food, that might have given a hint that this would be the last time the three of them would spend together? Perhaps it was in the way that Nanaboozhoo balanced the bowl on his knee, or in Ma'ingan's laying two small logs to bank the fire before he left, or in her, Nokomis's, usual invitation for Ma'ingan to stay the night; was it less sincere than usual? Whatever it might have been, and she thought about possibilities many times in the days after, it was not seen or paid proper attention, and Ma'ingan said his usual farewell, *giga-waabamin*, I'll see you again, as he left.

"Stay along the shore as you walk; it is hard to see where the ice might be thin," Nokomis said to her wolf grandson, although he was already so far that he wouldn't hear.

And it still happens this way sometimes, that a wolf will take the shortcut across the lake between points along the shore, perhaps from the boarding house in Canal Park, the last one standing now decades after Mickey and Louis and how many other *niijis* have walked the earth in the footprints of Nanaboozhoo. Each time there is an element of risk involved—will there be a random spot not thick enough to hold his weight, will the cold be overpowering to a wolf who may not possess a warm winter jacket, thick socks, insulated boots, even gloves or hat? Will there be a random moment when the mishibizhiig will sense movement above the ice and, exultant that Nanaboozhoo's little brother has strayed from First Street, away from the Bethel and the Union Gospel Mission, rise through dark lake water and ice heavy as their own hearts to repeat once again and seal the continuing fate of Ma'ingan?

THE HARBOR

As the traditional wintertime story of Nanaboozhoo and Ma'ingan is true, so is this fictional story of Louis and Mickey.

By mid-February of the winter after Japan's surrender, the surface of the Duluth harbor between the scrap yards and the grain elevators was covered by rolling snowbanks over an ice sheet nearly a foot thick, creating a direct route that cut the distance between the two sites by at least a mile. Because of the lake wind, however, which obliterated tracks and blew snow into crazed peaks and drifts that disoriented and exhausted the walker, few took advantage of the shortcut. Those who did were hardy, intrepid, and usually without streetcar fare. And from time to time periodically over the years, some years none, some one or two or more, the risk-takers became disoriented in the white vastness of the snow-covered harbor and walked out onto Lake Superior, where they became lost and were never seen again.

Louis, though, who knew the route between his boarding house at the edge of the scrap yards and Maggie's house back of Elevator D by heart and true love, walked the shortcut across the harbor even during snowstorms. When he finished work at the scrap yard on that late winter afternoon, he punched out and danced down the boardwalk under clear skies and a gibbous moon. Leaning into the wind, he walked back to the rooming house with Maggie's house across the harbor in sight; the harbor shiny and flat in spots where the wind had blown away the snow down to bare ice interspersed with snow blown into peaks that had become hard and crusty; the thinnest top layer thawed from midday sun and refrozen into an ice that when broken by those intrepid walkers without streetcar fare became sharp as a knife, cutting into any exposed fragile human skin above shoes and socks. Louis paused to breathe cold, deliciously crystalline air, with relish. "A beautiful night," he thought to himself with his true love on his mind and heart. "Wind's dying down; a good night to walk to Maggie's, if Mickey is feeling all right."

He walked past the rooming house to the edge of the harbor shoreline; peering through the clarity of icy winter air, he could just about make out Maggie's house, small in the shadows of the grain elevators; squinting, he saw the yellow light of her kitchen window, and the curtains, made from strips of men's old shirts from the St. Vincent de Paul rag bag, and a movement, perhaps her hand at the window, moving pieced plaids, stripes, and solid white fabric aside as she looked for him.

"I'll wash up first," he thought, "and bring Mickey with."

At the rooming house, he cleaned the bottoms of his boots out on the back porch and left them on the rug in the kitchen, next to the back door, to dry. The landlady watched him as she turned and pivoted from the woodstove to the table, from the sink to the pantry, heavy in the haunches but light on her feet, one eye on her work and the other on Louis, overseeing his walk across the kitchen floor in his stocking feet, cautioning him as always to make sure that his boots were back far enough so nobody would fall over them.

"Mickey around?" Louis asked.

"He's resting right now," she answered. "Swept out the back porch today, and brought in some wood. Shoveled the stairs, back and front. Tired him out. Bring him down with you; supper's about ready."

The door to the room at the top of the stairs was wide open; inside, Mickey was asleep, on his own side of the bed as always. His shoes were on the floor, on his half of a rag rug, his arms stretched above his head, knuckles resting against the brown-painted iron headboard. In sleep, he blew small puffs of air with each breath; his face looked animated. What did he dream, Louis wondered, and who was he this afternoon on that other side of consciousness, rabbit or wolf? He bent forward from the waist, peering more closely at his friend, who lately looked more alive in sleep than he usually did when awake.

"Give him a few more minutes," Louis whispered to himself. He stepped carefully across the floorboards, stifling their squeals to muted squeaks, removed his work shirt, which he hung from the doorknob, and took a bar of soap and a towel from the dresser into the bathroom, where he cleaned scrap-yard grime from his face, chest, and arms. When he returned to the bedroom, he stepped unintentionally on the whiniest floorboard, which woke Mickey, whose face with eyes open changed from the animation of his dreams to the weary, otherworldly scape of his earthly existence. He smiled; the slight curl of his lip reincarnated the waiting hunger of his youthful self, before those deadly red flowers of tuberculosis had begun to sprout, grow, and bloom in his chest.

"Ma'ingan," thought Louis. A wolf. So, Mickey's form this afternoon was that of a wolf, thin and with a dulling pelt but a wolf just the same, like Nanaboozhoo's younger twin. "Ma'ingan," he said aloud. "Miijim temigad adopowining. Gi bakade ina?"

"Nimbakade, aya; hungry, that's me."

"Wiisinii-daa, then. Thinking of stopping by Maggie's after supper to visit; you want to go with?"

"Sure, nice night out for a walk. How was work today?" Frail and unable to hold up to a physical job, Mickey asked most days about the scrap yard: who had sliced his hand on a rusted, broken metal trap; who had told his mother-in-law just where to get off; who had said what to the boss when the boss couldn't hear.

"Well, you know how Dulebohn says he's too old to shoot craps anymore 'cause he can't see good enough? Well, he's out at the Viking with Andre LaForce last night, and gets loosened up with just one beer, and he took these two guys, Andre says he never saw them before, doesn't know who they are. Anyway, he says Dulebohn purt' near cleaned them out . . ."

"Little old Dulebohn still outsmarting everybody at craps? Ha!" Mickey bent over as he laughed; coughing wetly and gagging, he pulled the rag he used for a handkerchief out of his back pocket and wiped his mouth and nose. "I'd have liked to see that!" he wheezed.

"Take it easy on yourself, Waboosoons." Louis used Mickey's childhood name. "You don't want to go coughing yourself to pieces. C'mon, let's go eat." He walked ahead of Mickey on the stairs down to the dining room. At the landing, Mickey rested one arm across Louis's back and leaned; bearing the weight of the wolf who was now a rabbit, Louis slowed their descent.

The landlady mashed a scoop of boiled cabbage and quartered potatoes onto Mickey's plate, then speared the leanest piece of salt pork from the pot onto the potatoes. "Have some bread, too," she said, "to sop up the juice—it's good for you."

Mickey thanked her in his shy way and ate steadily through the plate of food, using the bread to push each mouthful onto the fork. "Boy, this is good," he said.

"Best supper in town," Louis agreed.

"S'good for you," the landlady repeated. "Especially the juice; it loosens up what's in the chest." She was under the impression given by Louis that the new boarder was recovering from pneumonia and not the contagious and deadly TB. "Now, you boys are staying home tonight, aren't you?"

"We were thinking of going to Garfield, doing some visiting over there."
Mrs. Lukaszewski glanced over at Mickey.

"I was thinking that Mick, here, can take the streetcar, and I'll cross
over the bay."

"I'll walk with you, Louis."

"It's an awful cold walk, Mickey, even to the streetcar," the landlady
shook her head. "But if you're going to go out you can wear Emil's boots."
Mickey was the only person who was allowed to borrow her deceased husband's boots, which she kept on a mat outside the door when she was home
alone, to give the impression that there was a man around, a big man with
big feet who would thoughtfully leave his boots outside and step cleanly
over her shiny floors to the chair next to the couch in the parlor, where he
would protect his wife and home from any harm.

"Tell you what, we'll both take the streetcar out there and Mickey can
take it back; I'll come back from Maggie's across the lake." Louis picked up
the bonnet-shaped black iron coal hod by its handle and went outside to fill
it from the bin.

Helping Mrs. Lukaszewski, Mickey shook crumbs from the tablecloth
out the back door and then spread it back on the table with her flowered
tureen, a wedding present that had never been used for food, in its place
in the center. Back in the kitchen, he put on his jacket and watch cap and
stepped into Emil's large boots that he laced tightly at the ankles. "If you
don't need anything else done, we'll see you later," he said.

"You'll take the streetcar back, too, won't you." It was not a question.

"Will do." Outside, he watched her through the kitchen window, the
lit room bright against the winter evening; bent over the sink, she scrubbed
at the stewpot. He would save the carfare money to buy her something, he
thought; something she would never buy for herself, maybe a handkerchief
trimmed with lace, like Maggie's.

BECAUSE MAGGIE WAS HIS TRUE LOVE, Louis looked toward the lighted
kitchen window as he and Mickey approached the house on Garfield. The curtain was open, he saw; perhaps she would move back and forth in the kitchen
and he would see her from the back, the side, the front, unaware that he was
watching. Perhaps he would be able to tell if she truly loved him back by the
way she might place a saucepan of water on the stove to boil or the way she
might close the curtain, her hand, scarred from the work at the mattress
factory, tender as she closed the night away from the house, her thoughts of
Louis softening and smoothing out the deep line that creased the space on
her forehead between her eyebrows.

"Looks like somebody's home," said Mickey. At the top of the back stairs, he breathed in deeply and exhaled slowly.

"Cooling the pipes?' asked Louis, knowing that Mickey did so to ease his discomfort.

Mickey nodded. "Let's go in."

Louis opened the back door and entered the kitchen. "Anybody home?" A small boy ran into the kitchen, followed by a tall, stooped woman who squinted nearsightedly and blinked at the two men, who stepped closer. Recognizing their faces, she smiled and clumsily waved them toward the front of the house. "Biindigen," she said. "Come in and sit down—Mother is reading to us, it's a book about a girl who's in an orphanage, and she writes letters to this old man, she thinks he's old, who sends her money, and I think it's going to turn out that he is young and that he is really in love with her. I hope so, anyway. Did you like the book Mother read last week, about the debutante, that girl who went to balls but she didn't care about any of that because she was in love with a man who was poor, but it turned out he was really a duke and so her father let them get married?"

"The kind of story you and Maggie both like, hey, Girlie?"

"Oh, we do." Maggie's oldest daughter sighed happily as she led them through the hallway to the front room; behind her skinny haunch Louis thought, as he always did, that she reminded him of a female moose. People always said that she took after Maggie's mother and Maggie after her father, Half-Dime LaForce, who had, as the story goes, married Artense Jollineaux for what he had been told was her father's money. No wonder Girlie was so impressed by the library book that Maggie had no doubt checked out just for her. Half blind from the eye disease that she had caught at the Harrod boarding school, Girlie took as much pleasure in being read aloud to as other people did going to the movies. She must be close to thirty, Louis thought to himself, but she might as well be sixteen.

Maggie was sitting on a double bed in the front room, a quilt draped across her shoulders like a shawl and her feet up. In her stocking feet she rose to lightly embrace Mickey. "Are you cold, my friend? We were just going to make tea. Biik," she addressed the boy. "Go put some water on, will you? Are you done memorizing your catechism?" Her youngest child, the only one of her children to live at home and not at Indian boarding school, attended a Catholic school in the West End.

The woman sitting at the other end of the double bed looked up from a garment she was mending. "Biik's jacket has a ripped armpit," she explained, "and I'm setting this gusset in. Can't let go of it; I'm almost done." She frowned at the wad of brown corduroy jacket and at the diamond-shaped patch of brown wool she had set under the arm. "Try it on, Biik, and let's see how you can move your arm." She instructed the little boy to reach forward and backward, then straight up. "How does it feel?"

"S'good, Auntie Helen. I'll be careful to not tear it anymore."

"It looks like a new coat, sister," Maggie commented. "You always do such neat work, sewing."

Helen ducked her head modestly. "I always try to make things look nice if I can. Mickey, Louis—if you need mending done you can always bring it here, you know. What are you boys up to tonight? Come to hear Maggie read *Daddy-Long-Legs*?"

As Maggie read, the little boy and Helen worked in the kitchen, speaking in whispers in order to hear as the story of the orphan girl continued. Mickey listened with his head bent and his hands folded on his knees, murmuring every once in a while "mm hmm," as was his style when listening to stories. Girlie's head was cocked slightly to one side, the scars on her rather beautiful purple eyes sparkling occasionally as they caught the lamplight; she gazed unseeingly and raptly at the scenes that she imagined playing high on the front room wall.

The tea, though hot, was weak, and it was served with a plate of sliced cold lugalette. Louis ate his slowly, picturing Maggie's hands greasing the square metal pan with lard, then gently working the flour and water into a soft dough that she patted into the pan before placing it in the oven to bake. He let the top crust of his slice melt onto his tongue, the prints of Maggie's tender, work-scarred fingers dissolving slowly.

"Have some more bread?" Helen invited. There was one slice left on the plate. Louis had noticed a bowl of potatoes on the kitchen table and thinking that it might be all that Maggie had left in the house, declined a second helping. "Mickey, you still hungry? Want that piece of lug?"

Mickey glanced at the bread, then at Louis, who he thought surely would have liked to finish the plate of Maggie's cooking. Louis shook his head. "Biik, how's about you eat that last piece—you need it, you're growing so fast, be taller than your mother next time I see you."

Biik beamed and ate the slice of lug as Maggie resumed the story of the orphan girl and Daddy-Long-Legs. Much of the room, however, had begun to lose interest: Biik opened the catechism and reread his lesson, closed his eyes and mouthed memorized words. Mickey, seated on the floor, leaned his head back against the bed; his eyelids drooped and closed, and he snored lightly. Louis jingled the coins in his pants pocket; Maggie raised her eyebrows and he apologetically stopped. "Should we stop for tonight?" she asked.

"She sure is unlucky," commented Helen. "How many bad things can the lady who wrote this book think up?"

Girlie, in a disappointed voice, answered, "Hope things start going her way soon."

Helen half-snorted. "Don't worry; they will. That's the way it is in books. Not real life, though. In real life things would keep on going the same way and it wouldn't be a good story for a book at all. In real life they'd say she was one of those people just born that way, unlucky."

Maggie closed the book, a finger marking her place. "Does it ever make you wonder about people like that, how that happens that they're just born that way?"

"Some are born lucky and some are born unlucky," said Louis. "No reason, I don't think. Look at Noel Dulebohn—always likes to bet and just about always wins. He's smart, sure, but there's more to it than that. Then look at the Dommages—have you ever known any of them to not have bad luck? There's nobody gets bad luck like that, and all the time, unless they're born to it." Embarrassed, he remembered that Mickey's mother had been a Dommage. "Hey, Mickey; nibaa ina, niijii?"

"Hmm? I'm awake." Mickey coughed and then coughed again, deeply. "Is the book done?" he wheezed, and then caught his breath.

"I think these people want to go to bed—let's go. Time to maajaa."

"Stay if you want. Mickey, you tired? You can sleep here." Thinking of the two men snoring on the floor next to the bed where she slept, Helen stifled a sigh to herself.

"Naa, got to get to the scrap yard early, line up for the work," Louis answered. "Mickey's going to take the streetcar home."

The men put on their jackets and boots. Louis left first, but Mickey lingered another ten minutes because of the streetcar ride, which would lessen the time it would take to travel from Maggie's house to Mrs. Lukaszewski's. "Going now," he called from the stoop as he closed the front door.

In the kitchen, Maggie didn't see Mickey walk, not toward Superior Street, but toward the bay and Mrs. Lukaszewski's house on the other side.

FROM THE ICE-COVERED HARBOR behind Maggie's backyard Louis could see the ship canal and aerial bridge, gray in the moonlight against the snow-covered hills of Duluth. Although he couldn't quite make out Mrs. Lukaszewski's boarding house against the other houses gathered at the harbor shoreline, in all of the houses the city lights, Duluth's downtown, glowed above the unevenness of brick buildings.

On this February night Louis felt the coming spring in the air. "Daylight hours are getting longer," he thought. "Can't see the stars; must be cloudy in the sky." He inhaled deeply. "Might be getting up near the freezing mark." He rarely felt cold, and in Mrs. Lukaszewski's house, which she thriftily kept what the other boarders thought was on the cold side in winter, he sometimes felt too warm and sat outside on the steps for fresh air, even on below-zero days. As a child in the Miskwaa River settlement up north he had lived in a one-room tarpapered board house with his grandfather. They used the wood stove mainly for cooking, which was usually enough to heat the place; you could always burn more wood to warm up if you needed it, as his grandfather said. And why waste the wood if you didn't need to?

His grandfather had frozen to death the winter before Louis was sent to the Harrod Indian boarding school, not because the house was cold but from bad liquor. After trading a venison haunch to Frank Dommage for a bottle of home brew, he had walked out the door in the middle of the night; probably to pee was everybody's guess, and he had fallen facedown in the snow where he lay until Louis found him the next morning.

"The old man," Louis thought, "he was always good to me. And talk? He sure knew a lot of stories." From a house near the shore a dog barked and keened; in answer, another dog howled. He remembered a wolf howling years ago when he was still a boy, in that same pitch in the late afternoon before his grandfather died, not long after the Dommages had left. From somewhere out in the dark, deep woods he heard a howl, and then far from the other side of the house, another. Wolves, his grandfather explained. They'll stay away from you if you stay away from them. Call Pokey and let him in the house; they don't like dogs.

"Pokey looks like a wolf; maybe they'll think he's a wolf, too."

"Gawiin. Go call him and I'll tell you about it."

Louis opened the door. "He was waiting, Grandpa. I think he was scared."

"Here, old dog, sit down. You ain't a wolf, are you? Just an old *animoosh* wanting to come inside." The old man spoke slowly. "See, it's like this: *mewinzha*, a long time ago when things started out, Nanaboozhoo and the wolf, Ma'ingan, they were brothers; twins, in fact, and their grandmother, Nokomis, well, she was helping her daughter when the babies were going to be born. See, the first baby, Nanaboozhoo, when he was born, he was a little tiny white rabbit, and Nokomis put him on the floor underneath a little birchbark basket to keep him from hopping away while she helped her daughter with the second baby. When that one was born, it was a little wolf, Ma'ingan and it's a sad story. The girl was having a real hard time and her mother was beside herself; she threw Ma'ingan out the doorway of their little birchbark hut and tried to help her daughter, but the girl died.

"So Nanaboozhoo was raised by his grandma, and they didn't see Ma'ingan again for a long time. The brothers met when they were little boys and Nokomis wanted Ma'ingan to come live with them, but he didn't; he was happy to know them and they got along, but the circumstances, how things went when he was born—well, he didn't have any hard feelings but how it goes is, you can't change what happened and can't help how you feel.

And Ma'ingan, when he died, it could have been Nanaboozhoo but it wasn't, instead it was his brother, and wherever he is, Ma'ingan, you know he isn't mad . . . Mii 'iw for tonight." The old man had stopped there; as was his way of doing things, he would continue the story when the time was right, maybe the next night or another night.

Louis dropped his cigarette butt into the snow and looked across the bay, empty and covered by ice and snow. "Mickey must have got back to the house," he thought.

BACK OF MAGGIE'S, Mickey stood at the shoreline and stepped onto snow-covered ice, his feet warm in Mr. Lukaszewski's boots. "Like summer," he thought, wiggling his toes. "Late summer, like when we had to leave Maggie's and walk to the train to go to Harrod school."

Mickey walked lightly on warm concrete, a city sidewalk, his paws tapping a silent rhythm that left no prints. Behind walked his cousins—Girlie, Bud, George, and Vernon—resigned to grief yet hopeful, two carrying a lunch for the journey and extra clothing, one holding the hand of a small boy whose round face was shiny and stretched with crying, the sun in captivity. "Wewiib. Ma doesn't want us to miss the train." Bud hoisted the smallest boy up onto his back.

They quickened their steps and Mickey became the wolf, leading the pack to the depot. Through his thin-soled boarding school shoes his paws felt the hardness of hot concrete toward the train depot, the silent pattern an unrelenting and unforgiving song repeating itself in his head and heart, one day one day one day. In the spring they would retrace the steps but in reverse, their time at boarding schools breaking season to season, life to life, Maggie's children and Ma'ingan created as everything else was to draw breath and appear, to fulfill a purpose, to leave. And what of their time at Harrod—surely their purpose there would be to witness, to remember.

Mickey's feet, warm as summer in Mr. Lukaszewski's boots, stepped onto the frozen bay. They would take a shortcut to the depot, he thought, and not miss the train.

And so that February evening the wolf who was also both waaboos and Mickey loped across the ice-crusted frozen bay, his paws tapping a silent rhythm so light that they left no prints. As he ran, a cloud drifted from the face of the moon that, rising, eerily exposed shadowed drifts and peaks of snow, then an expanse of whiteness and beyond that the lights of the houses. He saw the way so clearly, the frozen white terrain reflecting moonlight past the blackness of night sky to the stars that grew to glittering flowers that bent in their heaviness toward the earth. In those contrasts of light and dark, Maggie's shingle-sided house was the color of the sky, the light in her kitchen window a yellow, small and weak in the shadows of the grain elevators that had become columns that changed from white to invisible columns and back again as clouds again drifted across the moon. So, too, Ma'ingan's coat changed its hue back and forth, back and forth as he ran past elevators A, B, C, D along the shoreline, in and out of shadows the color of Lost Lake on a summer night, in and out of light of the white of snow, ice, and stars. He ran, thinking of Maggie's house and of Maggie, Louis, Helen, and Biik inside; the kitchen light would go out, and they would sleep in the sweetness of each other's presence in the little shingled-sided house. He ran, camouflaged by his coat that changed colors under the shifting light of moon, star snows; he ran through night air that cooled and soothed his chest and lungs so that his cough became a memory that could possibly never return. And halfway across the bay he thought about what a pleasure it would be to smoke a cigarette in the midst of all that beauty of light and shadow, stars and moonlight, snow and ice and the twinkling lights of downtown, to smoke a cigarette without wheezing and coughing and spitting, and so he paused to light a match, inhaled to suck the flame into the end of the cigarette, and felt the cloudiness of smoldering tobacco sink down into his lungs, where it entered his bloodstream that it lit as brightly as the surrounding bay.

"Sugaswaa," he said lovingly to the little fire at the end of the cigarette.

Beneath Ma'ingan's feet, beneath the ice where he stood, mishibizhiig, the lake spirits, turned their faces toward the glow above and the outline of Mr. Lukaszewski's pair of winter boots. In their silent underwater way of speaking, they recounted to each other old stories of conflict and revenge, of Nanaboozhoo and his younger twin, Ma'ingan. Of the sacred promise made to the memory of the ancient one, leader in generations that ruled the lake long before the memory of mortals: his death would be avenged, and avenged again. The cold hearts of the Oshkii-Mishibizhiig heated and the surface of the frozen bay softened. Wait, the oldest and most experienced said in his underwater voice, as red winter suns throbbed within their large ice-gray bodies, and they maintained their patience as the cigarette burned its way down, as the glow of orange fire dimmed and died. Biizindan, commanded the oldest; they listened as Ma'ingan coughed deeply and sighed and then as the soles of Mr. Lukaszewski's winter boots began to move, the *steps increasing in speed as Ma'ingan resumed his lope, now heavier and tiring, toward the shore.*

He grew cold and ran. He ran, boots now feeling like the concrete of winter; ahead, the lights of the houses near the shore seemed to grow no closer but soon he would see them, or should he turn around and go back to Maggie's? Would they hear the heaviness of his breathing that was now becoming a wheeze, a whistle, and would they look out the kitchen window, unable to see him but waiting? Home, he thought. Home. Ma'ingan's lope grew uneven and ragged; the boots, sinking through the crust of ice over snow, blemished its shining expanse of whiteness with prints that ringed his legs, just the tops of the boots, and chafed his ankles. Panting white puffs of breath, he turned and saw, he thought, Maggie's house just up ahead, kitchen window again lit, a brighter yellow now, the moon lighting the railroad tracks along the shore to the color of the stars.

I'll be there soon, Ma'ingan said to himself. To settle his nerves, he stopped to roll another cigarette.

Almost there, he thought as he struck the match.

And the lake spirits who had followed the outline of Louis's boots broke the surface to once again seal the doom of Ma'ingan, the little brother of Nanaboozhoo. The story was true then and it was true when Mickey, who bore the spirit of rabbit and wolf, repeated the encounter; that is how it was then and how it still is today.

WOODS LOVELY, DARK, AND DEEP

THE WOODS OF NORTHERN MINNESOTA are beautiful and mysterious, wondrous and dangerous, all at once. As there is a world of water-breathers under the surface of Lake Superior, there is a world in the forest of air-breathing diverse beings—trees, flowers, medicines; animals, birds, insects, each with its own qualities of design, purpose, and ways of living.

There are many stories from the forest about the interactions of these woodland beings with one another and Nanaboozhoo, and lessons to be learned from every story. However, the most seemingly simple and evident lessons are multifaceted, with depths and complexities as well as darknesses that may not be understood or even considered until after the story has been heard many times, and perhaps not even then.

An aspect of Anishinaabe worldview rooted in the traditional values is an ability to see and accept ambiguities and contrasts: one story is true and so also is another, Nanaboozhoo is both wise and foolish, the atmosphere in the forest is lovely, healing, destructive, and frightening. In the big picture, perhaps these things all balance out, and balance is a quality of Bimaadiziiwin, the living of a good life. The ongoing education of an Anishinaabe whose life journey is on that path involves listening for what they can learn from traditional teaching, reflecting on that, experiencing and trying out for themselves, and then becoming the storytellers/sharers of knowledge. That education surely involves not just the desire to learn but the humility to remember that it is unseemly to think that one single person should strive to know everything.

Many people know a little, some people know a little more, and we are all part of something larger than ourselves.

Gaagoons

A story that I love very much is about Gaagoons, the little porcupine. I have heard it many times, but sharing the story, telling it to others, involves more than memorizing the order of events. It is even more important to remember the points that must be included in each telling, and where those points fit into the story. In listening to it repeated, I drew close and let the recounting wrap itself around me; it has become something I wish to pass on to others who I hope will do the same. Like all who tell a story, my means of passing it on reflects my own ways of communicating while returning again and again to the pieces that must be included.

Mewinzha, a long time ago, Nanaboozhoo and Nokomis lived in birch-bark huts next to each other. They had chosen a location that was within the shelter of the thick forest yet was close enough to Gichigami for its water, ease of travel by canoe or over ice, and because they loved looking at the lake. In the forest was plenty of food—game, medicines, berries.

Everything they needed had been provided by the Creator, which eased any worries Nanaboozhoo might have had for his grandmother's well-being while he was gone for his destined work, which was to walk the earth. On a late spring morning Nanaboozhoo rose early, as he had been taught to do by Nokomis, said his morning prayers of thanks, and built a fire to heat water for raspberry tea, his grandmother's favorite drink. Before leaving for the day, he made sure that that Nokomis had enough food, water, and firewood; she reminded him to not forget the skin bag in which he kept a length of rope twine, a knife, and a ball of pemmican.

As Nanaboozhoo headed into the woods, he sang, in the beautiful voice that he had inherited from his mother. Nokomis watched lovingly until he disappeared into the thickness of the trees and bush, listening with some apprehension as the song faded. She said to herself that she would hear it again when he returned, at first very faint but become louder and more full as he grew closer to home. Yet the woods were so dense and could be dangerous, even when Nanaboozhoo's wisdom and prudence prevailed over his occasional poor judgment or foolishness.

Some distance inland, an extended family of porcupines lived in an area of the forest that was isolated and quiet. Gentle and timid, they chose that place because it was away from some of the more aggressive animals. Nokomis and Nanaboozhoo were friendly with the little community, loving them for their sweet, kind nature: the Creator had gifted them with a softness of spirit and body, with the softest long fur that waved gently in the breeze as they gracefully waddled through their daily chores. Nanaboozhoo was especially fond of one of the young porcupines, who he often picked up and held in his arms just to be close to that sweet softness.

On that fine late spring morning, the grandfather of the porcupine family sent Gaagoons, the young friend of Nanaboozhoo's, on an errand that would take him away from their sheltered home out into the woods.

Gaagoons had been taught to listen and watch for animals who can be aggressive and mean. He knew to leave the pathway and stay behind thick trunks or leafy trees, out of their sight, to stay still and quiet, even his breathing, and he knew to walk quietly, carefully not rustling any foliage, in order to not call attention to himself. Grandfather had confidence in the young porcupine's ability to do these things, and that little Gaag would of course feel some apprehension—but a little apprehension and caution can be a good thing, and he kept his grandfather's instructions in mind. Leaving the safe, comfortable little porcupine settlement, he waddled carefully, setting each step down lightly, listening and watching. The further he traveled into the density of the forest, the less sunlight shone through the trees, and the ground became damper and more muddy. Gaagoons began to wonder if he heard breathing and, if he did, was it his own? No, the sound was from in back of him. He sped up his steps and the breathing grew heavier, deeper, quicker. Afraid then to look back, he waddled faster; the breath grew hot on his hind legs and became a growl, then more than one growl.

The growls turned to howls. "He's getting tired!" "Get him!"

Gaagoons broke into a waddle that was as close to a run as he could make it, but the others were gaining on him. He dove under the low branches of a prickly bush at the side of the trail and wrapped his body around the base, straining in the muck of mud and wet, dead leaves to get closer, his body a circle. The predators, larger than Gaagoons and unable to get past the scratching branches to the base of the bush, swiped at him with their claws and paws and then gave up and left, laughing at the pitiful, frightened little porcupine.

Gaagoons waited until he could no longer hear the predators before rolling out from under the bush. Just as he was about to pull himself upright, however, he heard another sound—this a beautiful song in Nanaboozhoo's voice floating through the damp, fragrant air of the forest. He considered rolling back into the mud under the bush, then thought that his grandfather would of course expect that he would greet his friend and so stood in the middle of the trail and raised a paw.

"Boozhoo, aaniin ezhi-ayaayan, niijii?" His voice was a little weak and embarrassed-sounding.

"Gaagoons! How wonderful it is to see you out here, friend. Nimino-ayaa, giin dash?"

"Oh, fine . . . How is Nokomis? I hope that she is well."

"Very well, and she will be happy to know I saw you. And your grand-father?"

These courtesies when on for a while, as Gaagoons had many relatives. Finally, after everyone had been asked after, Nanaboozhoo paused. "Gaag,

I can't help noticing that you appear to be in a situation of some kind. Can I be of help?"

At Nanaboozhoo's kind words Gaagoons felt greatly relieved. Near tears, he began to explain about his errand, and the predators, and the escape into the mud.

"They were laughing at me, Nanaboozhoo, and I don't blame them." He held out his front paws. "Pathetic. And I can't even run fast enough to get away; instead, I hid under that bush, rolling around in the mud. No wonder they think I am a coward, and deserving of their ridicule. I am of no use whatsoever, can't even run an errand for my grandfather; how disappointed he will be when he sees me."

Nanaboozhoo's heart ached for his friend, whose tear-filled eyes shone sadly as they reflected a shaft of sunlight that penetrated the thickness of the pines. He reached down to pick the little porcupine up, marveling to himself at the amount of mud that one small body could collect. How to comfort Gaagoons? "Don't talk that way about yourself," he said. "You know how you are regarded by Nokomis, how greatly we appreciate your kind ways and sweet nature. Surely you and your family are a wonderful example for all the beings in the forest."

Gaag's mouth quivered.

"Oh, my, he really does feel bad," Nanaboozhoo thought to himself. Placing the porcupine back on the ground, he stood him up on his hind legs. "You look much taller," he said.

"Really?" asked Gaagoons, then wobbled and fell onto his side. "It's no use," he said.

"Cleaning up might help," Nanaboozhoo thought to himself. He picked Gaag up again and held him gently, comfortingly, pulling bits of mud from his paws and under his chin.

"Weweni, be careful to not back into that bush," said the porcupine. "It is quite scratchy."

"It is, isn't it?" Nanaboozhoo broke a thorn from the bush and stuck it, sharp end out, into the thick layer of mud covering Gaag's back. "Not just scratchy, it is actually very sharp." He broke off another thorn, and another, and more, sticking them into the mud, until the porcupine's back was covered, and then set him back onto the ground. "My, you look very fierce—how does it feel?"

Gaagoons flexed his back. "It feels wonderful."

"You are a warrior; a warrior, indeed," admired Nanaboozhoo

Gaagoons smiled modestly. "Miigwech, niijii."

The two friends went their separate ways on the trail, Gaagoons listening to Nanaboozhoo's song until it faded into the forest.

On the way home Gaagoons once again had the feeling that he was being followed. Nervous, he sped up, but again felt hot breath at his backside. He was about to run when the predators growled and screeched, "It's him again—get him good this time!"

The largest of the predators leaped into the air and right onto Gaag's back, and then screamed in pain, rolling onto the muddy ground. "Run! Run for your lives! Gaag is going to kill us all!"

The predators ran away, and Gaag was left alone to finish his errand. When he returned home, his family was surprised at his appearance, which they admired very much. He told them about his adventure with the predators, which they admired even more.

"Gaag, you will be our protector from now, a warrior and hero to all porcupines."

Gaagoons smiled modestly.

Not long after that he was introduced to the daughter of a porcupine family that lived even deeper in the forest. She had a beautiful and kind disposition, and he was a warrior protector, a wonderful match. They found that they were suited to one another, and fell in love. The next spring, their first children were born, all with that soft sweetness that is the nature of the porcupine, and soft fur that as they grew became quills on their backs. And porcupines have had quills ever since that time. They have kept their sweet nature, but are rarely bothered anymore.

And Nanaboozhoo? I expect that when he returned home that evening, Nokomis had a hot meal ready, and that they talked about his day as they ate.

Windigo Bimose

At the end of that last summer
    that last summer we were like you
when even the pines could give us no shade
and their brown, sharp needles, paler each day fell
    at first, I thought the sound was rain
and lay lifeless where they fell,
where they cut and scratched our feet till they swelled

at the time of day that no shadows were cast
a piece of fire fell from the sky
and the sun grew on the ground.
Ravenous, it began to eat the earth.

Carrying babies, grandparents, the infirm
we fled, for a time ahead of the smoke and flames

but after the dry hungry summer
we were in a weakened state, even
the strongest. One by one we made the choice
to continue alone or die with our families;
    I cannot fault one's decision to stay
    or another's to abandon
for myself, after my old parents, my wife
and our children all but one fell like pine needles
I chose to walk with my firstborn.

My oldest daughter who'd always been
strong as a man and slow to tire
walked beside me for how long
    days, nights, lifetimes.

When she tripped and fell, the others
    fewer in number
    than the fingers on both my hands
watched without hope or interest
    would I have done the same if I were them
her struggle to stand, singed lids closing
slowly slowly over dulled desiccated eyes.

As I lifted my firstborn my heart recalled
    her birth, her mother
    her small brothers and sisters
    her grandparents
and tore. Rent, it spilled and emptied.

Then from the void my hunger emerged
    much like the sun's
and through the air less smoky now I smelled
from the north a corporal warmth
    a young mother's arms and breast
and heard from the north a lost child's cry
    young bones and skin tender
    ice-cut feet bleeding into snow

Follow me; let us walk, I said to the others.

Ravenous, I lifted my daughter.
Ravenous, I carried her across my shoulders.
Ravenous, I stepped the first step

follow me; let us walk
and then ravenous, the remnant rose and followed.

We had fled from heat to live in the cold,
endless cold our dark and everlasting life
where we never slept again, and where
in endless appetite we search for you
    your warm breath
    your blood that flows bright and steams
    in icy winter air
    how we despise your frailties, envy your strengths
    how we love and hate your living flesh

how we yearn and crave past death
past life we hunger, and we walk today.

I WRITE HERE about a spirit of the woods, frightening to think about yet created, as are all beings, with reason and for purpose. The spirit, Windigo, is not often talked about, though in popular culture outside of Indian Country I have seen reference to it, usually not very well informed and usually reimagined as horror-story monsters made in the image of Hollywood and comic book entities. The being is presented as imaginary, contained in fiction—or as a psychosis, or even as some sort of myth, like the troll under the bridge or the witch in the Hansel and Gretel story, who lived in the woods. There was place up the North Shore some years ago called the Windigo Lodge; it burned down, I recall. This is not a spirit to be taken in any way but very seriously. There are not many stories about them; most take place in winter, and are told during that season, if they are told at all.

These are entities that crave human flesh that, when consumed, increases their size and their appetite. They are always starving, then, always on the hunt. Windigog are fearsome beings, larger than human beings, unclean and unkempt; there may be blood, dried or fresh, on their faces and around their mouths, or bits of flesh. They are thin, skeletal until they eat, which stops their cravings only temporarily because that terrible sustenance causes them to grow larger again, and to need more to maintain. They do not desire the flesh of animals, though they will eat them as a last resort if they cannot find a human. Their real hunger is for human flesh and that is what they hunt, using their sharp eyesight and even sharper sense of smell. Lifting their heads, they inhale delicately yet deeply, discerning the direction of warm, human breath, perspiration, and body fluids. Catching the scent, they move quickly toward the prey; there are stories of the ground shaking and leaves trembling, dishes rattling on a table, vibrations in the air, and birds flying to the highest branches of trees, calling out a warning. Because windigog can run at superhuman speed, there is not much time for the hunted to flee, and not all escape.

The kill leaves evidence—blood, a piece of torn clothing, a dropped knife or tool.

It is possible, I have heard, to kill a windigo by pouring boiling lard down its throat, or with fire. There is a story about a woman caught between her house and a windigo when she was outside cooking food that had been stored for winter. With nowhere to run—and how could she outrun such a large and ravenous being?—in desperation she grabbed the iron kettle of melting fat from its hook over the fire and dashed the contents at the monster's face; her aim was lucky and most of the lard went right into its open mouth. Shrieking in agony, the windigo collapsed and died, its insides melted from the heat of the lard. In another story, Nanaboozhoo almost outran a windigo with his superhuman speed; however, the windigo gained on him. Tiring and slowing, almost out of breath, Nanaboozhoo circled back to his own campfire, leading the monster around the far side of a large mass of rock. Once past the rock, Nanaboozhoo zigzagged back into camp and leaped over the fire. Too late to dodge the flames, the windigo fell into the fire and burned to thousands and thousands of pieces, which drifted upward in the blast of heat. Scattering in every direction, they became mosquitoes.

The old Ojibwe stories have many reasons and purposes. History is remembered and recounted, listeners learn ways of working toward Bimaadiziwin, the good red road that is the living of a good life. Listening, we gain appreciation for the past and strength for the present and future. And the stories are entertaining—the creation stories, love stories, ghost stories, stories of hilarious things that happened to someone's uncle that one time—and sacred, all of them.

Debwewin. The stories are true, and how they are received or regarded has no effect on that. They are here for a reason and a purpose, their destiny and how they came to be determined by the Creator. We don't always understand why and we use the word *aaniish* rarely; perhaps our knowing these things is not meant to be, as the old Ojibwe would say. There are some theories that windigog are here to teach us to not be greedy, that greed begets greed, that we must always be careful and mindful of what is around us. We have seen windigog presented in movies and cartoons as fiction, and written about in literature and psychological studies as metaphorical, but those are only mankind's limited and feeble, even unseemly, efforts to pursue knowledge. Windigog exist because that is their destiny as determined by the Creator. And I could be wrong, but I do not think that they are soulless.

They had a beginning, they are here.

RABBITS WATCHING OVER ONIGAMIISING

Nanaboozhoo was conceived in violence yet carried and birthed by the gentlest of girls; there is mystery in this contradiction. There is physical evidence of his walk on the earth from the smallest hawkweed blossom to the forests of Bois Forte, from the tiny bits of rock that agate lovers find along the North Shore to the Point of Rocks that overlooks Duluth. His destiny was as large as the world, yet he started out as a *waaboosoons,* a bunny, and when I see a rabbit I think of Nanaboozhoo—it could be him, after all.

Here in Onigamiising there are two types of rabbit, and one is actually a hare and not a rabbit. The cottontail rabbits are smaller, with puffy white tails and brownish fur that stays the same color through all seasons of the year. Snowshoe hares are bigger: they have large hind legs and furry feet, which gets them over the snow easily (like showshoes); their fur turns white in winter, a natural camouflage in the north. When we see a rabbit in winter it is almost always a snowshoe hare—but that is a scientific difference that might be only a fine point in the eyes of the Creator. We know from traditional teachings that all animals are important to the earth, that no animal is ranked higher or lower than any other in eyes of the Creator, and that all have a contribution to make. They are humble beings who have given us food and clothing (soup, meat, broth, hats, mittens, blankets, tools) and they don't take much in return—but they do love garden flowers. One late June after they had eaten the tulips I had planted next to the garage, I sprinkled some blood meal around the rest of the flowers to keep them away. Although the backyard attracted hordes of flies, it did work temporarily. The bunnies, who were no doubt watching me reproachfully from the brush back of the yard, waited patiently for rain to clear things up for the delectable petunias that bloomed wildly from the blood meal that had soaked into the ground. The next year I planted marigolds, which the rabbits nibbled on, but not much. It was a good compromise, I thought. We are all here to live our lives; marigolds are easy to grow and pretty as the dandelions that dot the grass all around the house, small flower faces that honor the sun.

It was a friend who told me about the rabbits watching over us. We were at the Tweed Museum of Art looking at a painting by Jim Denomie of a white rabbit. She asked if I had ever seen rabbits sitting on top of the snow outside in the middle of the night, in wintertime.

"I have," I answered, "just a few times when I couldn't sleep. It was on clear nights, rabbits in moonlight sitting not upright but with their legs folded underneath, like a cat. I wondered what they might be waiting for."

"Do you know what I heard? That when we see them like that at night it is because the rabbits are watching over us, over a sleeping world and our dreams."

It is a comforting thought, that of rabbits keeping watch in the quiet darkness. Since then, sometimes when I am awake at night I get up and go to the window to look outside. When I see them, it is always on winter nights, and always by moonlight. Each time, I think that I might stay at the window looking at the rabbits for hours—might one of them be Nanaboozhoo? But then I remember that they are to keep watch and I to sleep, and so return to bed.

Across the bay that connects Lake Superior to the St. Louis River, my daughter, Waaboosoons, who is now a grown woman with a family of her own, sleeps in her bed—I hope sweetly and soundly, watched over by the rabbits, who are the embodiment of Nanaboozhoo and her childhood namesake, whose purpose it is to do that.

PART IV
TRAVELING SONG

THE END AND RENEWAL OF THE EARTH

How things happened with Nanaboozhoo is that he was born of the First Daughter and the North Wind with a destiny that was determined long before memory of the spirits, and that was to walk the earth. Much of the natural world we know today has been formed or altered by the encounters he had while on his travels—the woodpecker has a crest of feathers standing upright on the top of his head, the bear has a short tail, migrating birds fly in a V formation. The mud hen has short legs and red eyes. The world ended in a Great Flood and was redeemed by the muskrat, humblest of animals. That redemption repeats itself daily in all our lives.

The Great Flood came about from discord between Nanaboozoo and the mishibizhiig, the lake spirits, when Nanaboozhoo was a small boy living on the lakeshore. He enjoyed skipping rocks, those flat, round stones that if thrown just right will bounce several times on top of the lake before they sink. Such a satisfying sound they made above the song of the waves; the boy thought that a bigger rock might make a louder sound, but found that the larger the rock, the less likely they were to skip. He began to throw larger rocks into the water, and to climb on the large rocks that rose out of the lake. Dropped or thrown, the sound was delightful.

Nokomis saw what her grandson was doing with the rocks and cautioned him. "Boonitoon, leave those heavy rocks alone. Don't throw them in the lake, and stay off the big rocks. There are spirits living in the lake, the mishibizhiig. That is their home, and they don't like being bothered."

Nokomis's words made the game even more attractive to Nanaboozhoo, and he returned whenever his grandmother was not watching and continued, trying to lure a mishibizhii out of the water. When that finally happened, the excited boy increased the teasing, tormenting the spirits who rose again and again to the surface. Each time, he ran away from the shoreline a little frightened, but more bold as he grew to young manhood.

One afternoon an annoyed mishibizhii spit a wave so high that it knocked Nanaboozhoo off his feet. He shouted, "That is not funny!" and threw handful after handful of rocks angrily into the waves, which sprayed them back onto the young man, and what had begun as teasing became rancor that continued for a long time and grew into a mutual hatred. Eventually, this deep conflict led to the death of Nanaboozhoo's twin, the innocent Ma'ingan, who was dragged into the lake by the mishibizhiig as he loped over the ice on a winter night. Nanaboozhoo avenged his brother's death by tricking, then killing, the leader of the mishibizhiig, who retaliated by causing a Great Flood that covered the earth.

Everything was lost except for a few survivors who floated on a raft on endless water. Nanaboozhoo was one of these; what a terrible lesson he was learning. How could life ever be returned to the earth and the beings who had now suffered such devastation?

REDEMPTION

After the great flood and long before the memory of mortals, Nanaboozhoo and four animals floated on a raft looking for a surface upon which they could live and walk. Amik (Beaver), Ojiig (Fisher), and Nigig (Otter) each exhausted their strengths diving to find where the ground originated, but they were unable to stay underwater long enough to find the bottom. As they despaired, the last and smallest animal, Wazhashk (Muskrat), asked to take a turn. Nanaboozhoo and the other animals told him that it was hopeless and not to try, but the muskrat insisted. It is because of the courage and sacrifice of Wazhashk that the earth was renewed.

Wazhashk, the sky watched this.
Mewinzha, long before the memory of mortals,
Wazhashk, the sky watched your timid, gallant warrior body
    deliberate and then plunge
        with odd grace and dreadful fragility
    into translucent black water,
    dark mystery unknown and vast as the night sky
and barely—to a single inhalation shared by a weeping four
and a hopeful splash quieter than an oar—break the surface
    into concentric expanding disappearing rings as
    water circled your departure,
    for a moment transparently covering
    amethyst soles tiny seed pearl toes
    above that determined small warrior body
    that hurtled from sight, then
    in an instant was pulled into cold dark depths,
    seeking the finite in the veins of a waterlocked earth.

Wazhashk, the water covering the earth watched this.
Mewinzha, long before the memory of mortals,
Wazhashk, when you were obscured from the sky

the water watched you
    lost from the sight of the praying four
    alone on a small raft afloat on vast water
nearly faint under crushing cold
    alone then below the waterline
    seeking the finite in the veins of a cumbrous earth
    as waterfingers intruded and invaded
    all unguarded aspects of your small warrior body
    now stiff and graceless, pulled by will into icy dark depths.

Wazhashk, in that dark mystery
unknown and vast as the night sky
you continued your solitary plunge
    lost from the sight of all who lived above water,
    who considered your size and your courage
until in cold and exhaustion your silent voice whispered
    ningosh nindakamj
    nindayekoz niwiinibaa
    I am frightened I am cold
    I am tired I must sleep now
and was heard by the Great Spirit.

Wazhashk, you were heard and were answered
    mangide'en, anamiindim mangide'en
    gaawiin gimbezhigo siin
    anamiindim mangide'en
    have courage, have courage in the depths
    you are not alone
    have courage, have courage in the depths
till your spirit roused and spoke
    geget geget
    through my despair I will

and the Great Spirit watched this and guided you.
Mewinzha, long before the memory of mortals,
Wazhashk, the Great Spirit guided you and watched
    your small curled brown fingers
    stretch curving cinabrese claws
    to grasp the muddy, rocky breast
    of a waiting Mother Earth.

And today, Wazhashk, hear us breathe
our inhalations and exhalations a continuing song

of courage sacrifice grace redemption a continuing song
since long before the memory of mortals.

With each telling of the story with each singing of the song
we once again rise to break the surface and seek
the finite beyond the grace of this merciful Earth
the finite beyond the mercy of this graceful Earth.

Since then, we Anishinaabeg have for countless generations also been born to walk in Nanaboozhoo's footsteps: we are part of the circle and continuity of existence. *Debwe,* it is the truth that what happened in the past, in the old days of Nanaboozhoo and thereafter, still happens today and is still *debwewin.* There is a different story and walk for every Anishinaabe—but we are bound to Nanaboozhoo and to each other by our shared destiny that the constant batterings of history have burnished to an existence that shines.

MISHOMIS

MY GRANDFATHER, LIKE NANABOOZHOO, was a being both magical and flawed, one of those Anishinaabeg who walked the places that Nanaboozhoo had, their footprints layering their generation's stories on top of the others before them on the rocks over which Misaabekong formed and grew. They are part of the many-faceted record of the physical and spiritual, which are really not separate at all, that the old-time storytellers share by beginning "*Mewinzha,* a long time ago . . ." In listening with ears, mind, and heart, we begin to see the same way things happened in the days that the moon's grandson traveled over the earth, and in the way that things still happen sometimes today. The physical forms may change, but the truths, the realities of Nanaboozhoo's destiny and ours, do not.

Here is how it happened for my grandfather, Elias, who appears as the man called Louis in my fictional work.

During the times of the Great Migration, some of Elias's grandparents and their ancestors before them traveled from New England to Quebec to Ontario and then south into Minnesota, and some from the southern route, from New England to the southern side of Lake Superior to Mille Lacs and then north. By 1850, the families had become part of the settlement next to the American Fur Post in Fond du Lac, which today is the furthest western neighborhood in Duluth. After the 1854 treaty established reservations, they were relocated to the Fond du Lac Reservation. According to the annual Indian Census records of that time, they were next removed to White Earth, which was intended to eventually become the combined, only Ojibwe reservation in Minnesota. That never happened. Some of the extended family remained in White Earth, where they received land allotments and became members of that tribe; others moved back home—my grandfather's family returned to Fond du Lac, where they received land allotments and became members of that tribe, then moved to Mountain Iron, Minnesota, back to the Brookston area of Fond du Lac, and back again to Mountain Iron. As was common in those times, Elias and his siblings were removed from their family and sent to various Indian boarding schools—the Vermilion Lake Indian School, where Elias met my grandmother Victoria; Pipestone, in southwestern Minnesota; and Haskell, in Lawrence, Kansas. As it was for many families, not all siblings attended the same schools at the same time; the boarding school system was organized while it was haphazard, and Elias was not always able to live at the same school as family members. At Pipestone he learned both harness making and to work in a print shop; he was athletic, a fine baseball player, and a chronic runaway. My grandfather never did finish school: the last entry in the Pipestone Indian School records that mentions him lists him as a "deserter" when he was seventeen—but I know that his education as an Indian, as Anishinaabe, was precious and ongoing throughout seven decades of a life that began in the middle of federal assimilationist policies and ended in 1970 when he had just turned seventy and I was almost twenty, near the beginning of the AIM activist days but almost twenty years before federal termination policies would be ended by Congress.

How things happened long ago seems magical to us today: the Creator made the earth and everything on it—the waters, the lands, the beings that swim, fly, walk, the spirits, and finally human beings. The stories of how the world was created and how things came to be the way they are today are the stories that anchor our history, beliefs, and ways of existing. "*Mewinzha* . . ." they often start out, a long time ago—and that is how the Anishinaabeg continue, by listening to the stories, often many times until they become part of one's own heartbeat. The beauty in this is profound.

But beauty manifests itself in many ways, and by that I don't mean the flip side, or reverse of beauty: I mean the intertwining of what are the loveliest and high-minded of our stories and heritage with those parts that might not be seen or thought of as aesthetically pleasing. Nanaboozhoo is a powerful spirit who still walks among us; in various stories he was selfish and foolish, kind and wise, mischievous and vengeful, jealous and altruistic. Crass, with a beautiful spirit. Generous, protective, petty but with a great heart. And that is the story of so many Anishinaabe people; my grandfather Elias was one of these. As are we all, each in our own ways.

Debwe, it is true that magical things happened long ago. *Gaye debwe*, it is also true that magical things happen today. One line into my typing the draft for this page in February 2020, my computer chimed a signal that meant a new email had arrived. The address looked familiar, I thought. I clicked, and it opened.

GRANDFATHER-IBAN GI-BIMOSE

WHEN I WAS IN MY MID-TEENS, on a summer day my grandfather Elias walked to our house from downtown. The house we lived in, where my mother still lives, is set close to the road but down a steep slope, and my parents kept the front rather overgrown. Whoever came to the front door walked down steps; surrounded by greenery, we would see first the feet, then legs, body, and finally the head of the visitor, and that is how we saw Elias that afternoon. Nanaboozhoo-like, he emerged from the thickness of green maple leaves overhanging the front steps and stood at the front door. He looked tired and warm, just like someone would who had walked from downtown to up the hill—west on First Street, past the Bethel and over the Point of Rocks, up the hill to Twin Ponds and the Skyline Boulevard's spectacular views of central and western Duluth, up the steepness of Piedmont Avenue, and then winding Springvale Road to our house. To visit. And he looked like he had been drinking.

My mother opened the door and he leaned slightly against the frame, thinking about all he might say. There was so much. It came out as a question. "Is Jerry home?"

"He's at work." My mother looked upset as he walked into the dining room, weaving slightly and oddly gracefully, and sat in a rocking chair.

"How are all the kids?" he asked. "How is everybody?" He sighed and rested his head against the back of the chair, circled by small children. And repeated himself again.

My mother told me to get him a glass of water. He drank it slowly, asking me "How's school?" while in the kitchen my mother was on the phone calling my dad. She came back to the dining room with a plate of cookies. "I'm waiting for your dad to call me back," she whispered to me.

While Elias asked the children their names, and repeated them back, trying to keep a half-dozen names attached to a half-dozen little faces, the phone rang. "I'll get it!" my mother said as she grabbed the phone from the kitchen wall and went around the corner to the basement doorway to talk (this is what we did for privacy in conversations—our phone had an extra-long cord for that reason). When the conversation ended, she pulled me into the kitchen and whispered to me that someone was coming to get him. "Somebody he is living with, out in the country, I think."

"At the work farm?"

"No, somebody who's taking care of him. Like a foster home."

For the next half hour he sipped water and ate cookies, an old man with so much to say and not knowing where to begin, wanting to be with us, his grandchildren. "How's school?" he would ask one of my sisters; to one of my brothers, "Which of you boys are boxers?" He asked about their training, their fighting weights. So much to say, impossible to know where to begin.

A car pulled up in front; we heard the doors shut and then two teenagers, a boy and a girl, emerged feetfirst from the maple leaves that hung over the front steps. They stood at the front door smiling. "We're here to give Paddy a ride."

Now, how did Elias know these two white teenagers, both so pleasant and confident, so tall and healthy-looking? What connection could he have to these strangers, so at ease and comfortable-looking and courteously unapologetic, with teeth as nice as their clothes? How could they, kids really, be in a position to tell my grandfather what to do? I felt defeated and helpless as they walked with my grandfather to their car, which was a clean-looking nice shade of medium blue. Who would be caring for my grandfather as though he was in a foster home? He was close to seventy; certainly his years should have earned him the prestige of elderhood—for probably the hundredth time in my life I wondered what had brought us all to that point.

As they drove off, the teenagers in the front and my grandfather in the backseat, he lifted one hand to wave at us. They couldn't possibly know how he looked at the world, how intelligent he was, that even in captivity his spirit was unusually special, and at the time I was of the opinion that they hadn't earned it.

My grandfather, I knew, shone brighter than the northern lights. He could speak Ojibwe; he sometimes did with my father, but not with me. He knew the traditional ways; he had been a hoop dancer, my dad had told me, with beautiful powwow clothing, and carried a dance stick with a bird's claw on it that had significance to him. He had beautiful handwriting, and he knew so many things about Duluth, and our family, and Ojibwe people, that he would speak about shyly and in such a soft voice. He hadn't lived with my grandmother Victoria since the boys were small, yet he was on good terms with everyone, always nice to people. He worked in the scrap yards, or at odd jobs, had played trumpet in a circus for a while, and had been a cowboy. He loved Victoria, and his own mother and dad, who had also parted company decades earlier but remained friends; he was willing to help people. He knew the woods. At a very young age he had been removed from his mother, as were all ten of the children, and sent away to Indian boarding school. He was an Ojibwe elder who carried the knowledge and wisdom of elders before him disguised as a vagrant in old clothes. And he was being driven away in the backseat of a nice car by a teenage boy and girl who clearly had some kind of control over his existence.

Still, he shone. I waved back in the same way he had waved to us, lifting one hand.

That was probably in 1966 or 1967. My grandfather died in 1970. It was more than a half century later that I opened an email and found that, as it turned out, there was a girl just my age at that time who had seen from another perspective what I saw and had thought about it a great deal, also. There was more to the story, more to the walk.

My grandfather Elias, on the left, with his brother-in-law
and nephew on a rooftop

PLACES REMEMBERED, THOUGH SOME HAVE CHANGED

February 2018

Dear Linda,

I have thought about writing this note for many years, but I didn't know who to send it to or what to say. Recently, in looking at some very old pictures with my sister, we came across one that sent us into an evening of storytelling and warm memories and ultimately some online research to find the "who" this long thought about note should go to. I chose to send this to you for a number of reasons and sincerely hope that you will be receptive to what I am about to share with you . . . but I will understand if you are not.

Elias (Pat) LeGarde (your grandfather, if I've done my research correctly?) lived with my family for a number of years back in the 1960s. My entire family grew very fond of Pat and he was such a help to us all! In addition to running our big household (he always had an apron on and I can picture him cooking and vacuuming and helping my mother, always a big smile on his face), he helped my dad with projects big and small, as Pat was a wealth of knowledge and skill—roofing the cabin, building a sauna, making a new road—all things that Pat was able to lead the way on. I was a tomboy and already loved to hunt and fish when Pat came into our lives. I spent MANY weekends with him at our remote cabin learning how to hunt better (it was not unusual to be woken up by Pat at 4:00 a.m. to have a huge breakfast, then off into the woods we would go in the pre-dawn, to return after dark to a cabin smelling of Pat's homemade baked beans). He taught me once to make a bow, and I think my sis and I still have miniature birchbark canoes that he made for us. He was so smart and so knowledgeable of the world around him. He set the course for my life in so many ways, from his storytelling that piqued my interest in so many things to his examples of hard work, living simply (but well!), and his humbleness. He was truly a beloved grandfather to my family, and most especially to me.

I see that you are a writer, and I know I will enjoy reading your books soon! I am an aspiring writer, with stories that need to come out. I have spent much of my life living in the woods and continue to strive to be self-sufficient—Pat inspired traits that have richly filled my life.

My sister and I would love to meet with you and any of Pat's family that may be interested to share memories. We both live near Brimson, so could easily meet in Duluth.

Kate

* * *

Kate, thank you so much for getting in touch with me. I would love to meet and to hear about my grandfather. Much of his life was hard; you probably know this. Many years ago, sometime in the late 1960s, on an occasion that he came to our house he was not in very good shape. A couple of young people came to get him and bring him where he was staying— might that have been you?—Linda

* * *

Thank you so much for getting back to me Linda, it is so good to hear from you and that you are open to meeting!

Yes, that was likely me (probably with my brother) that came to pick Pat up that day. There were many days like

that over the years until one very sad day that my dad said
"no more." So yes, I am aware of the hard life he lived. My
sister and I have always said that, knowing the hard parts
of Pat's life, we have always felt like we want to share
with his family the good parts that we were lucky enough to
experience.

My sister and I are both retired with very open schedules
and would love to meet up anytime that works for you and any
other family that is interested. I will leave it with you to
suggest a time and place and will look forward to hearing
from you in that regard!

Kate

* * *

WE DIDN'T MEET FOR TWO YEARS—the email conversation became buried
in my work files; although I searched for it a couple of times, I was unable to
remember her name, or when it had been sent. Had I erased it? I wondered.
Was I concerned about an intrusion into a life that the teenagers in 1966 or
1967 would not have been able to understand? And who owned my grandfather's story, anyway? Surely not me, I concluded, and so a year and a half
later I searched again for that email, again couldn't find it, then went into
old Facebook messages, in case that is where she had contacted me. Finally,
I posted a message on my own Facebook page and, three months later on a
night that she couldn't sleep, Kate logged on to her Facebook page; astonish-
ingly, my posting popped up. She sent another email and we agreed to meet.

We got together right before the shutdowns of the coronavirus pandemic began. The coffee shop was in the Kenwood shopping center, which
is a few blocks from the house where she had grown up and my grandfather
had sometimes stayed, as well as the Kenwood school, where I had learned
about Christopher Columbus as well as class and privilege and that their
limitations could not contain knowledge and truth. Kate walked toward me,
a small, mild woman, tentative in her movements. Mindful of the coronavirus, though not yet aware how the Perk Place and many other places would
soon close and reopen on a very carefully limited basis, we took care to not
touch or get too close as we sat across from each other at a large table, me
with my back against the wall (a habit picked up from my dad, who said he
did that because of Wyatt Earp) and the two sisters facing me.

We began carefully and visited for nearly two hours.

The story of Kate and my grandfather Elias, whom she knew as Pat, his nickname, is hers to tell and not mine. She has thought about him a great deal and may decide to write about that in depth herself, sometime; that is her part of the story. I will say that much of what she shared coincided with and filled out some details of his life during the mid-1960s. Their family's connection with Elias ended because of his alcoholism. At that time, Kate was in her mid-teens—and on the other side of history and the Point of Rocks, so was I. When Kate was told that he had died, she felt an unfinished business that she was probably too young to understand, and that is why she emailed me. My heart ached and sang at the same time as she spoke.

What Kate wanted to tell me was that she remembers my grandfather and always has. He met Kate's father, a policeman, when he was incarcerated, and helped the family around the house and their cabin for a few years. She said she wanted me to know that they had appreciated him, respected him, and to share some of the details about their family life during the days he became part of it. My grandfather knew the woods, she said: he could hunt and fish, knew quite a lot about the trees and plants. He could cook. He was helpful and kind; above all, he was humble. From time to time, he talked about my grandmother, Victoria, and about his two sons, my dad Jerry and uncle Tommy, both boxers; he was so proud of them, she said. And he had gone to an Indian boarding school, but when he mentioned it, he said nothing more. The memory saddened him.

I thought it might make Kate feel better to know that yes, Elias had had a funeral, that people came, relatives and friends from both my mother's and dad's side of the family. That we went to an aunt's house afterward to get together and have something to eat. That though she and I knew my grandfather from different perspectives, we each saw the complicated, many-faceted beauty that was his existence. I don't know if that helped or not.

A few days later Kate emailed a photograph to me, her dad and Pat, as she knew him, framing a sauna that they were building at the family cabin. My grandfather is wearing a blue plaid shirt and a red buffalo-check hat. He is kneeling, looking up at the photographer. The expression on his face is how I remember my dad: quizzical and at the same time knowing things that I don't.

That may have been the last picture ever taken of my grandfather. It's a good one, though, and I have looked a number of times for anything I can see beyond the split second of the camera click.

My grandfather, on the left, and Kate's father
COURTESY OF ALICE RUNNING

MY DAD ALMOST ALWAYS kept the window on his side of the truck open an inch or so as he drove, even in winter. I never asked him why; I think he liked the fresh air, and the sensation of not being completely separated from the outside. Neither of us would talk much as he drove and instead listened to the radio set on the "Music of Your Life" 40s and 50s station; he occasionally hummed or sang, very softly, short snatches of lyrics. If he wasn't in a hurry, he often took an indirect route to the destination—a stop at the painting contractor's shop, before he became a contractor himself, to see if there was work today; or to the DECC, the Duluth arena downtown, to pick up my mother after her work at the concession stands. Once in a while, after he went to work for himself, we'd stop at a house or business where he would give an estimate on a paint job—turning onto the streets that would take us across the Point of Rocks, or around Enger Tower, or past West End neighborhoods. The combination of outside air coming in the driver's side window, music, the places we passed created an atmosphere in the truck that I can only describe as contemplative, my dad revisiting places and times and me paying close attention as I wondered and tried to see what he was seeing. This was part of my education, separate from formal schooling, as Ojibwe people have been positioned in both.

My grandfather died at the hospital on a late October afternoon here in Onigamiising, brought there after he was found in the alley on First Avenue East between Superior and First Street. Conscious when picked up, he didn't say what had happened. He was able to tell them my dad's name. When my parents got to the emergency room he was gone—pneumonia, the doctor said, and that they thought he might have fallen or, more likely, been pushed down by someone who took his money. He still had his wallet, with my graduation picture inside but no money. My mother, Patsy, who can spin straw into gold and is about as tough as they come when she needs to be, identified him, to spare my dad.

There was a funeral, as I had told Kate, at Dougherty's, who were considerate to a family with many children and little money. There were no banks of flowers, there would be no car processional to the cemetery, but other than that the funeral director had created as dignified and nice a setting as for anyone's beloved relative. My grandfather wore my dad's clothes, his sport coat and pants, shirt and tie. Bronze-skinned and white-haired, he looked distinguished in the way that so many older Indian men do in death. There were friends and relatives at the service; there was kindness there, and respect for my grandfather's life and family. Afterward, we gathered at an aunt's house where a great-aunt lived with her daughter, Elias's niece.

My grandfather is buried in the Calvary Cemetery in Duluth, not far from his mother Ella and Victoria, who I believe he continued to love all his life. Close by also are my father and his younger brother, Tommy; further away are Victoria's mother Lucy Ann and, past that, my sister's husband, and Carmie and my grandpa Louie. In the adjoining Polish cemetery are my mother's family: her mother, aunt, baby sister, and other relatives. We visit there sometimes to brush off the markers of those who have markers and to acknowledge the space of Lucy Ann and Ella, who don't. This year several tiny hawkweed flowers bloomed on Ella's grave, their orange faces toward the sun, and perhaps me.

HOMELAND

I CAN ONLY SMILE WEAKLY when a nice person wants to tell me how they admire the Indian people because we are so spiritual and so close to the land, not because these things are not true—they are—but because they are profound and complex. What is an appropriate response, I have wondered, in much the same way I wonder what might be an appropriate response to the land acknowledgment statements our universities have developed in the past couple of years? What might be an appropriate way to respond to a statement that the speaker is standing on Native land that is no longer ours but theirs? My dad might have said, cheerily, "Why, thank you!" in a way he had that left the speaker feeling a little off-balance and wondering.

Ojibwe people are, indeed, spiritual and close to the land, for both religious and legal reasons. Onigamiising and the places that surround this place of the small portage have been our homeland, a vast area that was greatly reduced under the terms of the 1854 land cession treaty. Land that was returned to the bands as part of the treaty, the reservations, is intertwined with our legal identity as Indian people.

A very simplified explanation of how our legal status as members of a federally recognized tribe in relationship to the land: treaties were negotiated and signed by representatives of the bands. The reservation lands, at first owned by all members of each individual band, were later, under the Dawes Act, divided into individual parcels of land that were allotted to individual band members. When the Minnesota Chippewa Tribe was formed of six Ojibwe bands in northern Minnesota in 1934, the tribal roles were based on allotted Indians and their descendants. Later, blood quantum requirements were added. Marriages to spouses outside of the MCT, kinship lines, loss of land due to sales, taxation, swindling, or a combination of all three created complications that continue this day. Land passed out of many families' hands completely, yet they maintain their lineage (and often shrinking legal blood quantum) in the tribe; other families did not lose their lands but instead continue to own it in fractions that grow less and less with each generation. My family is like the latter; my grandparents and great-grandparents were allotted parcels of land in a place that was already homeland, and most of these have not passed out of our hands but are instead owned by many, many descendants. I think that is a blessing, actually, and hope we can maintain our fractionated status. After all, this is the land on which our ancestors lived and died, not only on their allotments but earlier than that, when they arrived during the Great Migration, a holy journey. We have been here so long that we are truly a symbiotic product of the land, our bodies and those of the ancestors sustained by the water, the harvest, and the hunt of what was placed here by the Creator for that purpose. When we die, we return to the land, which makes us part of the land and the land part of us.

Looking out from the Point of Rocks, we see homeland; looking deeply into the land and water, the sky and the horizon, we begin to see the past that is always behind the moving, fleeting present. Walking, we are on a trail broken by the ancestors' footsteps, invisible now but everlasting. Pondering, we think of the man who emerged from the rock blastings of Little Italy not much more than a century ago and made his way along the westward side of the Point to a group of schoolchildren and their teacher. Within this mystery are perhaps keys to understanding the reasons for the redemption and renewal of the Earth, and our purpose.

Maagizhaa, perhaps, if that is meant to be.

TRAVELING SONG

THERE IS A SONG for when someone is going away, in this life or going into the next, that sends the traveler off with a prayerful wish for a safe and happy journey. The song has just one line with words; the rest consists of vocables, those sung syllables that carry the melody, blending with the voice of the drum that runs throughout.

I think that the traveling song is one of the most beautiful in the world, and the story about the song is deeply touching to soul and spirit of those who hear and sing their good wishes and blessings to the traveler. The origin was from our brother woodlanders the Mi'kmaq, in Canada, who shared the song with the Ojibwe. Because of slight language differences and regional pronunciations and interpretations there are some variations to the song and the story. What I have learned about the origin of the traveling song from where I live, here in Onigamiising gaye Misaabekong, the place of the small portage and the giants, is thus:

A sweat lodge was constructed and the stones heated on behalf of a man who had been ill; weakened, he had become unable to walk. Friends and relatives helped him into the sweat lodge with great care because of his fragile state, and took particular care to keep him comfortable in his place of honor during the ceremony. They prayed for a long time, speaking and singing to the Creator their regard for the sick man, recounting all the good things he had done in the world and asking for consideration that his health improve. During this time, people of the family and community waited outside, adding their prayers into the food they prepared for when the ceremony was finished. The wait was long: children tired and slept in their mothers' arms, elderly closed their eyes to rest, leaning against their grandchildren; their patience and hope didn't diminish. After a time, the covering was lifted at the entrance to the sweat lodge, and the first to emerge was the frail man, who walked out on his own singing his prayer of thanks and praise to the Creator.

It is because of you that I walk.

When the traveling song begins, we stand to honor the traveler and also the drum, the singers and the song, and the Creator. We give the song and the traveler the best of our heart's wishes for safety and all good things. I listen to the song, and to the voices of the men on the drum, the sound a ribbon that floats and wraps around everyone in the room.

It is because of you that I walk.

My eyes meet those of a woman I have known since we were girls, then mothers, then grandmothers; from across the drum she smiles, recalling as I do other travelers and other journeys. Her lips move with mine as we breathe the words softly, so softly, below the singing of the men on the drum.

It is because of you that I walk, our silvery *mindemooye* voices sounding much the way the sky does when it sings.

ACKNOWLEDGMENTS

MIIGWECH: THANK YOU

to everyone at the University of Minnesota Press, especially Erik Anderson, who loves the timelessness of northern lakes and woods;

to Bob Swanson, elder, poet, and cousin who bridges generations as he walks and lives Bimaadiziwin;

to my grandfather Elias LeGarde and all whose lives he touched, and to his great-grandson Elias LeGarde, whose name carries our destiny;

and to my father, Gerald LeGarde, who told me that the most important word in Ojibwe language is *miigwech*, thank you, and that means everything.

LINDA LeGARDE GROVER is a professor of American Indian studies at the University of Minnesota Duluth and a member of the Bois Forte Band of Ojibwe. Her short fiction collection *The Dance Boots* received the Flannery O'Connor Award for Short Fiction and the Janet Heidinger Kafka Prize; her collection of poetry *The Sky Watched: Poems of Ojibwe Lives* was awarded the Red Mountain Press Editor's Award; and her novel *The Road Back to Sweetgrass* (Minnesota, 2014) received the Wordcraft Circle of Native Writers and Storytellers Fiction Award. She is the author of *Onigamiising: Seasons of an Ojibwe Year* (Minnesota, 2017), which received the Minnesota Book Award for Memoir and Creative Nonfiction as well as the Northeastern Minnesota Book Award for Memoir, and *In the Night of Memory* (Minnesota, 2019), which received the Upper Michigan Association of Writers and Publishers Notable Book Award and the Northeastern Minnesota Book Award for Fiction. She lives in Onigamiising (Duluth, Minnesota), where she was born at St. Mary's Hospital, within sight of the Point of Rocks.